Automated Share Trading Systems 2022

The Beginner's Guide: Making Money in the bullish, bearish and side markets

Contents

Disclaimer

It should not be assumed that the methods, techniques, or indicators presented in these products will be profitable or will not result in losses. Past results are not necessarily indicative of future results. Examples presented in this book are for educational purposes only. The representations in this book are not solicitations of any order to buy or sell. The author, the publisher, and all affiliates assume no responsibility for your trading results. There is a high degree of risk in trading.

Hypothetical or simulated performance results have certain inherent limitations. Unlike an actual performance record, simulated results do not represent actual trading. Also, since the trades have not been executed, the results may have under- or overcompensated for the impact, if any, of certain market factors, such as lack of liquidity. Simulated trading programs in general are also subject to the fact that they are designed with the benefit of hindsight. No representation is being made that any account will or is likely to achieve profits or losses similar to those shown.

Introduction

The decade that began in March 2009 was a good one for fundamental investment advisors. It's been easy in recent years for people to make money because the markets keep going up. But let's be clear: do not confuse a bull market with skill. Because it's been easy to make money for a while, people grow increasingly confident that the markets will continue like that.

However, our memories are short. Many traders forget what the market experience was like in 2008. And while in late 2018 we had a taste of what a downturn looks like, as of this writing in mid-2019 the markets are brushing up against all-time highs yet again. Sooner or later, bull markets come to an end. There *will* be a bear market. We do not know when. We do not know how big. But when it arrives, it will be ugly, uglier than most people expect. I am writing this book because I want you to have your investments arranged in such a way that you are protected and can profit hugely in markets of all types. To basically make yourself mentally immune from any kind of market movement, whether up, down, or sideways. Otherwise, it's very likely that you will lose some or all of the gains you have experienced over the last eight or ten years. Those gains could vanish in half a year.

The traders I work with have a common fear. You are afraid that you don't know what you are doing. You may be making some money. Sometimes you are up, sometimes you are down, but always you are afraid that the markets are going to turn, and then what the heck will happen? And what the heck should you do? You are afraid of losing what you have. Even when things are going up, you worry that a downturn is coming, and you don't know how to prepare for that.

Many of you who are reading this book have lived through a substantial downturn such as the one you saw in 2008, and while that memory may be fading, it's still there. You may have had an investment advisor, but those advisors usually do not outperform the benchmark when the market is rising, and when the market is falling you may well lose more than the benchmark. Yet you pay fees for this "performance"!

A Better Way

There is an alternative. In this book I am going to show you multiple, noncorrelated, quantitative trading systems that can make money regardless of the type of stock market behavior we are experiencing. If we're in a bull market, this approach works, and if we're in a sideways or bear market it also works. You do not have to be afraid of what the market is doing; you continue to accumulate wealth no matter what. In 2017, I wrote *The 30-Minute Stock Trader,* which introduced these ideas. Now, I will take you deeper into how to improve risk-adjusted return regardless of market conditions; and the power of understanding your objectives; and how to build systems according to your objectives, goals, and risk tolerance. In the following pages, I will show you how to lay the groundwork for building the right systems for you. This includes a deep, personal understanding of your own objectives and risk tolerance. By developing a clear view of your objectives, of what you want to achieve in regard to trading returns and risk profile, of how you want to trade long and short, of the style of trading that appeals to you, then you can build a system that suits your personality. That will be a trading system you'll stick to. A system that you will be executing consistently, with confidence and without fear or hesitation.

These are quantitative trading systems built on historic price data. Once the systems are built, you will have simple entry and exit rules, and ways to quantify how those rules perform against past markets to develop an exact statistical edge for certain systems in certain market types.

In particular, I will show you how combining these systems and trading them simultaneously improves performance exponentially. What matters is not the performance of individual systems, but the nearly magical effect of combining them for exponentially better results.

Perhaps the most appealing part of this approach is that, once you have established your strategies and set up your trading systems, you rely on your computer to tell you what to do. The emotion and fear that cause so much angst among most traders are not part of your experience any longer. The computer runs algorithms built on your values and beliefs about the market, and your comfort level with risk and reward. You trade daily, weekly, or monthly, based on what you want to accomplish, after the market has closed. Your computer does the hard work—you simply enter the orders (though that part can be automated, too; in fact I have mine running 100 percent on autopilot and many of my students have done the same).

This *is not* a handbook that tells you simply to do what I do in order to make money. Trying to follow what I do won't work for you, because you are not me. Your goals, desires, fears, and psychology are different. This *is* a book that first lays out the concepts behind my systems and what I do, and then shows you a complete suite of multiple trading systems you can develop. Nothing is left out. All buy and sell rules are revealed.

I am not trying to show you how to follow my systems. Rather, I am showing you how to use my approach to build systems that *you* understand, embrace, and will adhere to. As long as you execute your systems in a disciplined way, you'll have a statistical edge for making money. I will show you a quantified approach involving trading seven noncorrelated systems simultaneously that generated a compound annual growth rate from 1995 to 2019 of over 30 percent, but this is only an example of what you can achieve. It is a map of where you can go; you can and should find your own way using what I teach in these pages, rather than try to mimic what I've done.

Traders have experienced many different market environments in past decades. For example, there was the Depression from 1929 to 1933. There were huge inflationary environments from 1964 to 1982. There was the big crash in 1987. If we are willing to examine the past, we gain a good understanding of what *has* happened, but not what *will* happen. The future won't be the same, but it may be similar—or very different. Understanding what bear markets have looked like in the past, you might develop a system that would not have performed well over the last ten years. But when a bear market comes again, suddenly that system may save your financial life. Using a strategy of multiple noncorrelated systems, you'll be making money regardless of what the market does.

If what you are looking for is an automated trading system with quantified results, this approach will work for you. If you want to stop being afraid of losing in the markets, yet you want a statistical edge on building wealth, this book is for you.

However, if you find trading exciting, if you like to follow the news, if you enjoy the approach that most traders take of trying to predict what is going to happen, then this book is *not* for you. My systems are based on quantitative analysis, which looks backwards at market history to develop ideas about future market performance. It is the opposite of most trading approaches, which look forward, focusing on "fundamentals" to predict stock performance. The fundamentals approach is built on analyzing a variety of factors, such as growth and earnings, and making a decision. It is an approach epitomized by Warren Buffett and Charlie Munger. I have great respect for them, but I don't follow their path. I actually would like to know before I place a trade what the statistical edge is instead of using a more predictive method like stock picking, in which skill and decades of experience is so important. I work to understand and capitalize on historical price action, with no regard to the underlying fundamentals of a particular stock.

How I Learned To Trade This Way

I'm not a typical investment advisor. In fact, I'm not an investment advisor at all. I'm a self-taught trader. In the 1990s I had a whitewater rafting company in Mexico. Our family business in the Netherlands was a small venture capital firm—and it got into trouble. The advisors the firm had hired were not doing a good job, and there was a string of bad investments. My father called and said, "Listen, it's really going south, and we can't trust those advisors. I need somebody I can trust." There was quite a bit of money at stake, so I wrapped up my life in Mexico and came home to take a deep dive into the financials of that company.

I needed to educate myself. I don't have a math degree. I don't have a finance degree. But I've got a good brain, I'm incredibly driven and hard-working, and my father trusted me to turn things around. I was going to figure out how to do that.

There were two parts to the company: a venture capital arm that invested in different companies, and a stock trading arm. Within two or three months I determined that the investment bank advisors we were using had their own agenda and were incompetent. I fired them all.

I decided I had to handle the portfolio myself. This was right at the beginning of the dot-com crash of the 2000s. We were watching our past profits disappear, and the investment advisors we had on the market side were saying, "Laurens, don't worry, just stay with it and the market will come back." At the time I thought, "These are very smart people, they're from big banks, they've got big buildings, I should rely on them."

But I kept educating myself about what could happen, and I watched what did happen as companies like Enron and WorldCom, companies that had been promoted by all those advisors and banks, went to zero. I came to the decision that the risk-reward profile of the portfolio wasn't worth it. Against the advice of all the advisors, I went entirely to cash. That turned out to be a great decision because we were at the beginning of a bear market. We would have lost a great deal more than we did if I had not taken that step.

We were not making money yet. We simply weren't losing any more. By that point I had lost all trust in any kind of outside advisor. I had to educate myself fully to be in control and to find an investment approach that suited our family. I began taking trading courses and read upwards of 500 books about various investment and trading styles and tactics. I came to the conclusion that the only way I could actually trade something was if I had statistical evidence that what I was doing could actually provide an edge.

I came to understand that most traders and advisors base their decisions on fundamental analysis, which is simply a way of making an educated guess. For most of them, that will not work consistently in the long run.

I wanted evidence. That led me further into statistical, evidence-based trading with simple algorithms that could be programmed into computers. By using historical market data, I could see what the results of various approaches would have been if I had used them in the past. This gave me confidence that if I made *these* trades with *these* quantified rules, then at least I had an idea of what the possible statistical outcome should be if I traded consistently.

That led me to hire a programmer to program my ideas and backtest them. Basically, my ideas made sense. In 2007 I started trading using these algorithms, and I have been profitable every year, including the bear market of 2008. Remember, I had jumped into the family business during the bear market of 2000. I knew I needed systems that made money when the market went down—and that approach paid off in 2008 when we returned more than 80 percent in our family investments while trading with a low-risk profile.

My systems were rudimentary in the beginning. I didn't automate very much, and I began with only two systems, one for up markets, one for down markets. That worked really well from 2007 to 2011, when I took a big hit. The drawdown on the account really exceeded the backtested maximum drawdown I had expected. This is something that certainly can happen, but I realized I needed more systems to hedge against the market turning against a system and delivering an intolerably large drawdown. I also realized that if I have two systems and allocate 50 percent of my capital to each, if one system is not making money I can face a big drawdown. Yet I noticed that if I traded more noncorrelated systems at the same time, the risk of losing money was not as big. In fact, I was able to achieve a higher risk-adjusted return.

Let me underline this point, because it lies at the heart of this approach: by trading multiple noncorrelated systems simultaneously, *you statistically lower your risk and increase your return.*

Who doesn't want that?

Let me be clear. This is not a get-rich-quick approach. This is a get-rich-slow approach. It does not involve tricks. It is not a guarantee of any kind of performance. It *does* involve a good deal of effort upfront. And I have seen again and again that it works.

The more I learned, the more I refined my tactics. For example, from 2007 to 2011 I mostly traded a mean reversion (also called "counter-trend") system. But there were times when the market was going up and there wasn't enough volatility for that system to work well. I realized I needed a complementary system, such as long-term trend following. Over the years, the more I learned, the more I refined, and the more I saw that I needed multiple systems trading simultaneously. At the time, roughly a decade ago, my approach was limited by constraints in computing power. It takes a lot of computational power to run multiple trading systems simultaneously on a database made up of decades of daily market data from thousands of listed and delisted stocks. Few personal computers were up to the task until recently.

I began to teach what I had learned in 2013. I had come to like teaching when I was a ski instructor and whitewater rafting guide. I enjoyed watching students learn how to ski or to navigate a dangerous waterfall. I understood that teaching is the best way to improve my own skills. I also needed to pay for the investment I was making in program development, because I was competing with firms that had budgets of millions of dollars.

People ask me why, if I'm such a good trader, do I bother to teach? Simply put, because teaching makes me a *better* trader. The people I work with directly are some of the smartest traders I know. Their questions and insights challenge my thinking and force me to explain myself clearly—to them and to myself. Years of teaching have helped me eliminate flaws and errors in my systems and have honed my overall strategy. I enjoy helping people, and I improve my own skills and success. It's a great combination!

As a coach, my job is to teach you how to fish, not to give you the fish. Every student is an individual. I only work with committed people who want to improve themselves, to understand themselves, and to do the work. So many people want to get rich quickly. That's something that doesn't happen unless someone has a lucky run.

I wrote *The 30-Minute Stock Trader* because when I started my journey there was nothing like it. I spent seven years learning how to be a profitable trader and I wanted to write a book to show that you can make money in up, down, and sideways markets. I'm writing my second book to help traders understand the power of noncorrelated systems trading and to help them see how much risk they face if they are only trading long or trading only a few systems.

History repeats itself—we just don't know when. I want you to understand that what happened in the past is, in some form, going to happen again, so you can be prepared and can profit from it. In the following pages you will learn how to do that, so you feel better no matter what the markets are doing.

Chapter 1

Better Returns Regardless of Market Performance

By early 2008, many traders were feeling pretty good. The last six years had been a nice ride. Almost everyone wanted to get in on the party—or was already enjoying it. It seemed like the fun would never end.

We all know what happened next: the worst financial crisis since the Great Depression occurred. The financial system nearly collapsed after Lehman Brothers went bankrupt in September. The S&P 500 index dropped 56 percent in the months following. Traders who had been riding high woke up and truly felt like vomiting. Anyone who had the stomach to ride it all the way down lost half their money. Perhaps they lost a little less if they got out earlier, or a little more if they had to pay fees to those financial advisors telling them to stick it out.

Regardless, traders who were thinking about retirement realized they now had to earn approximately 100 percent after-tax return just to get back to where they had been before the crash. Those who rode it down, stayed in, and rode it back up didn't break even until 2013. That was a long five years, and it disrupted people's lives terribly.

Five years of being in a drawdown position causes enormous financial pain. People who thought they could retire instead kept working. People who had retired tried to go back to work, if they could find a job. People who were still working wondered if they ever could retire. The pain wasn't just financial, it was deeply psychological. When someone says, "I need to go back to work because my life savings are basically gone," they have experienced huge pain. Unless they were trading on the short side during the collapse—and the vast majority of traders were not—people were not protected. They lost a huge amount of money and didn't know where to go from there.

This wasn't the first collapse many traders had experienced—the last one had come just a few years prior. The factors behind the collapse in 2008 were complex and would take years to sort out, but the 2000 dot-com crash was a textbook case of boom-and-bust. As Internet stocks zoomed to new highs, traders who had no idea what they were doing got into the market. They didn't have any sort of investment process; they were participating in a mania that saw huge markups in stock prices from 1995 to 2000, not unlike the very first market bubble almost 400 years earlier, the Dutch tulip mania.

Manias are a byproduct of markets. The tulip mania was the first in the modern era, a speculative bubble among futures traders the likes of which no trader in the Netherlands ever had experienced, and which no one expected would ever end. At its peak, in February 1637, a single bulb sold could sell for ten times the annual salary of a skilled craftsman. By May of that year, the price had fallen roughly 95 percent. Once traders realized that buyers could not be found at higher prices, the market collapses.

In the late 1990s, everyone was talking about the stock market, and everyone seemed to be making money. Their neighbors and friends were making money, and they didn't want to be left out. In a fast-rising market like the one in 1999, there comes a time where investment professionals tell themselves, "Okay, that's enough. Now we're going to offload our positions." They engage in some profit taking, and the market starts to drop. The inexperienced trader doesn't recognize what is happening. He thinks, "I'll stay in—maybe I'll even buy more—because it's going to back up again, like it always does. That's what the investment industry tells us will happen."

Except that markets don't always go up. There came a moment in the spring of 2000 when 20 percent losses became 30 percent, and then 40 percent, and the worse they got the more people there were who couldn't take it any longer and threw in the towel. Some stocks lost 70, 80, even 90 percent. Every day, people were losing more money. They watched their accounts, they watched the news, until there came a moment where they could not even turn on the TV. They were afraid to look at CNN and see all those numbers in red. They were afraid to open their brokerage statements or go on their trading platform. They hit a point of maximum pain where they put their heads in the sand, said: "I can't take it anymore, I want to sell it all, and I never want to look at it again."

Bubbles and crashes are not uncommon. If you watched Bitcoin from early 2017 to late 2018, you saw a similar phenomenon: a huge runoff, followed by a massive selloff.

Bear markets, sometimes kicking off with fast crashes, are normal. In 1987, the market dropped 21 percent in a single day—and that was the index. Imagine if you were invested in stocks that were more volatile than the index. You could have lost 40 or 50 percent overnight. If you were trading on margin, you received a margin call. This created a catapult effect where more and more people were selling into a declining market.

The crash of 1987 was short-lived. It recovered relatively quickly. But it's very scary to turn on your computer and see that your stocks are down 20 percent. That causes pain, and pain causes panic. People felt they were losing money every minute and couldn't sell fast enough. They called their brokers and told them to sell at market, regardless of the price. Of course, that's the worst time to sell, but doing so stopped the psychological pain.

The crash of 1929 was much worse and lasted much longer. Before the crash, everyone was flying high. Traders made the mistake of confusing a bull market for individual skill. The pattern should start to look familiar to you: there had been a long runup during the 1920s, and everyone was talking about how well their investments were doing. When the market crashed, it came down hard. This was the first crash in which there was news of multiple people committing suicide because they had borrowed on margin, and now owed impossible amounts. What had seemed like free money evaporated.

The whole economy fell into the Depression. The Dow Jones average dropped 87 percent over four years. I promise you, nobody rides an 87 percent drop down and back up. If somebody had, it would have taken them 25 years to get back to where they had been in early 1929, not taking inflation into account. There was four years of terrible selling pressure. Nobody was talking about stock investments then. Nobody even wanted to think about them.

The popular sentiment at the end of the Depression bear market, from 1929 to 1933, was that the market would ruin you. The public's psychology completely flipped, from stocks being something everyone wanted to something that nobody would discuss.

The 1929 style of protracted crash is something we haven't seen for a long, long time. Crashes and recoveries in recent decades have been faster, generally lasting a year or a year and a half.

These scenarios happened in the past. Variations on them will happen again. We don't know when. We don't know for how long. We don't know how deep a bear market will go. We only know that it will happen.

Most people understand bull and bear markets. We can also experience sideways markets. From 1964 to 1982, the net performance of the Dow Jones Industrial index was zero. During those 18 years there was a 40 percent drop, and recovery too. Plus it was a period of high inflation. Interest rates ran between 14 and 17 percent in the late 1970s. If you had invested in 1964 and held on until 1982, your returns were flat—and you lost 75 percent of your purchasing power.

Most traders don't understand this history. They don't want to think about it. We all want to think about the good times. It's much better than trying to remember the pain of the downturns.

Common Trader Mistakes

When I begin to work with traders, many of them don't have a system that can tell them if what they're doing makes money. Several of my students have been portfolio managers who operated this way. They have read some books and they applied some rules that lead them to think, well, this makes sense conceptually. But they've got no statistical evidence that it actually makes money. That creates a lot of worry and uncertainty.

If they bought stocks, those stocks may well rise in value so long as the market is rising. But they have no idea what their portfolio is going to look like when markets go down. Their biggest risk, if they are portfolio managers, is that they will lose clients in a downturn. And they don't have any kind of evidence that their approach actually works. If a client says, "could you explain to me how your strategy works," none of them have specific rules or what to expect when the market does A, B, or C. They just know that when it goes up they probably will be fine.

Some traders look at a downturn and think they'll hang on. They say, "the last three times it went down it just came back up again. I'm just going to ride this out." The risk is that there will come a time when it keeps going down. A time like 1929, or 2000, or 2008.

Another mistake I see is people who have a little bit of knowledge, just enough to get themselves in trouble. They are a bit more active in the market. They will have part of a good strategy, but not the whole strategy. For example, they will make some money in a rising market. They know that they need to protect their profits, so they'll put a trailing stop-loss order on their stocks. Let's say they set it at 10 percent. The stock corrects 10 percent and they get stopped out—and then the stock starts rising again. Soon it's hitting all-time highs, and they feel (irrationally, but they feel this) that the market is against them.

Still, they don't want to miss the party, so now they buy in again at the top of new market highs. They have sold low and bought high. The flaw in their thinking is that while they understand the value of protecting their capital, which is good, they haven't properly calculated the volatility. If they had used a wider stop because they better understood what was going to happen, they wouldn't have been stopped out at the bottom of a temporary downturn.

The other thing they are missing is perspective. If you have a quantified system that has tens of thousands of trades in its backtesting database, even if you get stopped out at the worst possible time, you will be able to see that there is a statistical probability that this will happen sometimes. You won't think "the market is against me." Without that perspective, you'll feel like you repeatedly are buying and selling at the worst times. You start to play mind games with yourself, thinking, "how can it be that the market is out to get me?"

An additional issue most traders have is lack of consistency. They tend to go after the next best thing, and every time they are too late. They look at one trading system and see that is has had great performance in the past six months, so they want to be in that system. Most of the time they run behind the facts, chasing performance. That is a recipe for financial disaster. Trading these systems is like running a normal business—there are months when the systems don't make any money, but it's important to continue to perform the usual business functions so you are positioned to make money when opportunity presents itself. Investors need to do the same thing, but most don't.

Consistency in trading is key.

There are actually trading algorithms that capitalize on just these weaknesses in inexperienced traders. They know at exactly what point those traders will buy or sell, and they take advantage of that. They look at chart patterns. They can see where a stock looks very appealing and a lot of buying comes in, but then the buying stops and the stock goes down. The people who do not have backtested results chicken out and sell, and then it goes up again. Every time this happens the inexperienced traders are running behind the facts, and they can't help it. They can't change because they have no way to figure out what actually could work.

Why People Trade on Emotion

Why does this happen? After all, the world is awash in financial information, which seems to saturate the media. Here's what most traders don't understand, though: financial media institutions have an agenda that is not necessarily in your interest. Their agenda is to get as many viewers as possible so they can earn advertising income. They want to provide you with a lot of information that keeps you hooked. When the markets are down or there is a big sell-off, they make sure you see it. They show the panic on Wall Street. Then they interview their so-called advisors, although these are really just people who give opinions. They get sucked into the game, they may even believe what they are saying, but they are simply making predictions based on what they see on the TV.

Everything is in red on the TV, the charts are trending down, everyone is predicting what will happen—all of this creates enormous fear and anxiety in the trader. The trader doesn't know what to do. Maybe he should get out? What the broadcasting company wants him to do, though, is keep watching.

That's the most important thing. That's what their objective is.

The behavior of most traders is emotional, more emotional than they likely would admit. They look at their accounts, they think in dollar terms rather than percentage terms, and that makes them uncertain. They can't think rationally because, first of all, over at CNBC the talking heads are telling all these fear-driven horror stories, and secondly, the trader is thinking in terms of dollars that have disappeared from their accounts. Emotionality trumps rationality 100 percent in a situation like this. They get fearful and want to keep what they still have.

A mental state in which you are irrational, you are fearful, and you are hearing more fear from CNBC or the *Wall Street Journal* is the worst possible time to make a decision, because that decision is not based on logical analysis. It's based on what you are losing from your bank account. And people have terrible loss aversion. They can't stand losing. The truth is, in order to make money you need to be willing to risk money, and there are times when you lose money.

No matter how big someone's account is, you want more. And it's human behavior to constantly evaluate how much money you have and whether you are gaining or losing. The other trap you may fall into is looking at dollars rather than percentages. A 10 percent drop on paper can seem acceptable, but if you have a million-dollar account you tell yourself, "Damn, I just lost $100,000." Now imagine you have a ten-million-dollar account. Suddenly you lost a million bucks. It is the same percentage, but in dollar terms it makes you less rational.

I can see that in myself. When I started, I had a $30,000 trading account and I told myself I could tolerate a 20 percent drawdown while trading. That's $6,000. That seems okay. But let's say I have a $2 million account. Now 20 percent is $400,000. That dollar figure can cause you to completely change your mental position about strategy. Your strategy can be the same as when you had $30,000, the market move can be the same, but your perception about the situation will change because, in absolute terms, you lost more money.

How to Counter Emotions

This is one way even smart traders can fall victim to fear and irrationality. To counter that, we first have to use an automated trading system backed up by statistical results. Second, if we know the system is rationally designed, we can let the computer make the decisions about the trading process. We know we created the system when we were *not* feeling emotional, and the computer, of course, feels no emotions at all. It just executes based on the algorithm that represents the trading strategy. If that strategy is well designed to reflect your risk tolerance and you are confident that the algorithm has an edge over time, then you will do what the computer says. That's is the most desirable state to be in. The day-to-day price action of the market really does not affect you anymore, because you know you have systems in place to make money over time, regardless of what the market does.

For example, if the market is showing signs that it is going to sell off, you know you have systems in place to make money in that scenario. The market shift doesn't affect you, because you built systems that will make money when other systems are losing money.

I personally trade a strategy in which I have fifty combined systems, and I never worry about my positions or my trading. I have a very calm mental state because I have preplanned for everything that I can imagine could happen. In fact, my wife will never see my mental state altered, whether I am up or down. It is the long-term, consistent, positive expectancy of the system over two-and-a-half decades that gives me the peace of mind that this works.

In the coming pages, I introduce you to the systematized way of trading multiple, noncorrelated systems simultaneously that makes money in any kind of market. You don't need to trade fifty systems for this to work; I will show you how a handful of systems can achieve this result. When you do this, you don't live in fear of a bear market or some other market behavior. I will explain step by step everything you need to do and to have in place so that for any kind of market, you can have in place a preplanned system that handles it. If some of your systems are losing money, others will be making money.

My goal is to help you diminish or eliminate the fear you feel when trading.

That fear goes away because your uncertainty goes away. You won't know or try to know what the market will do; instead, you'll know you've prepared for it no matter what it is: bear, bull, or sideways. If you're making money with long systems in a bull market, you'll know that when the bear market rears its head your short systems will kick in. The net result is an improved result, regardless of market behavior, and, critically, less stress and worry in your own life.

Chapter 2

Why and How Noncorrelated Trading Systems Work

If you trade the way so many traders do, mostly in long positions, your investing life effectively is led by the news. Something happens in the world, so you turn on the TV or pick up the paper and hear that "this is a dangerous environment" or "traders have to be careful now." You pick up your phone and are bombarded by messages about the market.

This situation creates an enormous amount of stress, anxiety, and insecurity, because you are receiving all of this conflicting information and you don't know what to actually do about it.

Really, what are your choices? Everything that you see on the news is already converted into the price of a stock. If you want to trade according to the news, you're already too late.

You don't need to watch or read the financial news.

You don't have to. It's a wonderful feeling, because you don't stress out about what's happening. You don't have to rely on people who contradict themselves from one day to the next.

The best thing I ever did was to stop reading and watching the financial news. It was so good for my psyche. I can rely on the statistical power and knowledge of the reliability of my systems. Before I did this, if I had a long position in the market, I was glued to the television or my phone. I would be worried about a potential downturn. If I started hearing news about a possible downturn, my stress went through the roof. What should I do? Should I sell? Should I stay in? What's going to happen?

It was awful, and it didn't help my trading.

The trading systems you will build ignore the news. They are based on price action. We look at the historical price development of stocks and, based on that, we can define a buying decision and a selling decision. We quantify when to buy and when to sell. When you can quantify something, you can turn it into a computer program. Then you can test whether your approach has a statistical advantage—an edge that tells you it is statistically valid to buy or sell at a certain point based on the previous price action. When you know you have an edge, you can let the computer decide what to do based on the price action. Not based on the news. Not based on the talking heads on television. And, critically, not based on emotion.

This approach takes the emotion out of trading. Once you've built a system you believe in, the computer does the heavy lifting, calculating what to buy, and when, and what to sell and when. Let's say you've developed a long-term trend following system. You know the market conditions, when it will make money. And you know the conditions when it should lose money. Losing money is normal, and you understand that, so you don't worry about it, because when you make money you make more than you lost. That's the edge in your system.

Most of what is on the news every day is about fundamental investing—about looking at what the market will do. We build our quantitative systems by looking the other direction—at what the market has done. There's no statistical evidence for what the market will do, and so no comfort there. Trading where you have an edge and statistical evidence for it takes a lot of the emotion out. You have statistical evidence of what your maximum drawdown is likely to be, what your returns are likely to be, and you can be confident in that.

There are as many styles of trading as there are traders. However, to create a sound, successful multi-system approach, we need to concentrate on only four basic styles of trading: long-term trend following long, long-term trend following short, mean reversion long, and mean reversion short.

Long-Term Trend Following Long

In this system we scan the universe of stocks we are trading and look for stocks that are trending up. Perhaps we have set a parameter to look for stocks whose price is 20 percent higher than half a year ago. That could mean there's an upward trend. Another metric we might use is a simple moving average (SMA) where the stock has closed above the 200-day moving average. That's a simple way to quantify that the market is in an up mood. Once we buy, we want to stay in that stock for as long as the trend is going up. So long as the trend is up, you are making money.

When do you get out? When the trend shows signs that it is over.

This simple style means that you will be in profitable trades for a very long time, and at the end you have to be willing to give back some of your profits. You'd like to take your profits at the top, but you never know where the top is, so you stay in until the curve starts to bend decisively in the other direction. You'll set an exit point where it goes down and crosses a certain point. This might be a 20 percent trailing stop. When it moves down 20 percent from the top, you get out.

You need to be willing to give back some profit by having a relatively large trailing stop, so you don't exit prematurely on a slight downturn. If you are, you can catch those long bull market trends and ride the train all the way up.

Mean Reversion Long

A reversion system is the opposite approach. In the case of mean reversion long, you look for a stock that has been very oversold and for which there is a better than average statistical likelihood that it will rise back to its mean price. This is very short-term trading, where you get in and out again in a few days.

With an oversold stock you are buying fear, counting on the fact that the market has overreacted and will return to norms. When it does, you sell. With this system you'll have a lot of trades and a high percentage of winners, perhaps 60 percent of your trades. But you are only in a stock for a few days, so to make good annual returns you must execute many trades. This is very different from trend following—the perfect trend following trade is one that you enter and never exit; you just ride it up forever.

Mean Reversion Short

Mean reversion also works the other way. With mean reversion short, you seek stocks that have been overbought and short them, expecting them to drop back to their mean. There is a moment when what I call "stupid money" gets into a market, and the institutional money is heading for the exits. That's a sign that a stock is overbought. There's a statistically better than average chance that it will snap back to an earlier price, and that's when you take your profits.

Long-Term Trend Following Short

Trend following can work on the short side as well as the long side. When there are severe downtrends, as in 2008 or 1929, a simple system in which we sell short when the market shows a clear downtrend can be very useful.

These four systems are the core of our approach. As you will learn in this book, combining them can create very powerful overall systems.

How I Conduct Backtests

All the backtests in this book were done with a historical data set from 1995 to 2019. If you go back further than 1995, the quality of the data deteriorates. In addition, by beginning in 1995 we capture the dot-com boom and bust of 2000, one of the fastest boom-bust scenarios the market has seen. We also get the crash of 2008, the flash crash of 2010, and the big selloff of 2018. That large sample size is incredibly important. An inexperienced trader may backtest from 2017 until today and get great results. But then they enter a market environment that is very different from what their backtest represented, and they get very different results.

I use end-of-day data that includes the open price, daily high, daily low, close price, volume, and adjusted close, which takes into account stock splits (if you don't account for those the data skews). We don't want to base our systems on unreliable data, especially for short-term trading, because there isn't much margin for error.

You also want to be sure to have data that includes both listed and delisted stocks, so you don't have a survivorship bias. Take a look at the stocks that were listed on any of the exchanges, NASDAQ or NYSE in 2000: Lehman Brothers, Worldcom, Enron, Freddie Mae, Freddie Mac were all there. When stocks like those go to zero, or close to zero, they reach a point where they get delisted, which means they are no longer in any current exchange. Some of them don't trade at all. If you're backtesting only on the stocks that survived, and not including the stocks that failed, then the survivorship bias will skew you to a much better performance for your long systems than what would have happened.

Currently we test on a database of more than 40,000 stocks and about half of them are delisted stocks.

Stock splits have been taken into account. If you don't adjust for stock splits, you can have a stock that is $600 one day go through a four-for-one split, and the next day it's trading at $150. That can look like a terrible loss (or win if you trade short) if the system doesn't account for it.

I don't include dividends in my backtesting. You may not hold the stock at the moment it pays a yearly dividend, or the company may change its dividend payment or policy. This produces a more conservative approach on returns for the long systems, particularly for long positions in which you very well may receive dividends on stocks you hold for a long time. If you hold a stock for 300 days, you're much more likely to see a dividend payment than if you hold a stock for three days. In short systems you may typically hold a stock for a shorter time frame, so there is less likelihood you'd pay a dividend. Nevertheless, you'll pay one occasionally. By excluding any dividends, the combined results of our backtesting should be more conservative than live trading.

Make sure to include commissions in your backtest calculations. I estimate one-half cent per share and a minimum of $1 per trade, which is what I pay at my brokerage, Interactive Brokers, plus a very conservative slippage calculation. The point is to be as accurate and conservative as you can.

This 1995–2019 data set clearly shows a long-term long bias. It is a representation of the past, and it's useful for that. But we must bear in mind that the only thing we can know about the future is that it will be different. You could look at that backtested data and conclude that there's a long bias in the market over time, so if I run more long-term trend following systems, I should do better. That is true only in the past. We should trade as if we do not know what will happen in the future—because we don't. That's why I trade long and short in equal amounts, because there are times when trend following works, and times when mean reversion works. There are times when long systems work and times when short systems work.

We do not account for interest gained on cash balances. Although in the nineties the interest rates were a lot higher, currently at your broker you do not get any interest rate.

However, we do take into account paying interest rates when we trade on margin.

About Optimization

With current computer power, it is very easy to produce backtests that tell you more about the past than about their predictive value for the future. This is mostly done through over-optimization.

I have been very careful to choose parameters that are robust. For example, the table below represents some of the parameters and the results of a single system.

In this particular test, I use a simple moving average filter as one of the entry criteria. I chose, in this book, to use 100 days for the simple moving average. The table shows why.

In the table below you see other results of different numbers of days:

Table 1: Variable Simple Moving Average

Test Number	Days	CAGR%	Max Total Equity DD	MAR
1	70	21.75%	47.90%	0.45
2	75	22.41%	47.50%	0.47
3	80	22.87%	43.40%	0.53
4	85	22.76%	42.70%	0.53
5	90	22.53%	42.70%	0.53
6	95	22.50%	41.90%	0.54
7	100	22.52%	42.10%	0.53
8	105	22.88%	42.00%	0.54
9	110	22.88%	41.40%	0.55
10	115	23.57%	41.10%	0.57
11	120	23.99%	37.90%	0.63
12	125	22.66%	47.50%	0.48
13	130	22.55%	47.70%	0.47

What you see is that 100 days is right in the middle of very similar results (using the MAR as our criteria), which is a great sign of robustness. Whether we use 90, 95, 105, or 110 days does not matter. The results are almost identical.

You also see that there is one outlier, one moving average that produces a far better result than the others: the 120-day simple moving average, which has a MAR of 0.63. I could have easily chosen this number and shown you how great the system is. But that result most likely was due to a few better trades and randomness, which combined to create a better result. It would not be realistic to show that best number as a fair representation of the system. Also, an approach like that is a way of fooling ourselves, because we produce something that we perceive to be better than it really is.

In this chart you can see that the peak MAR of 0.63 drops off quickly on either side, quickly falling to 0.48, well below the robust 100 days MAR.

Chart 1: MAR Ratio as Simple Moving Average Varies

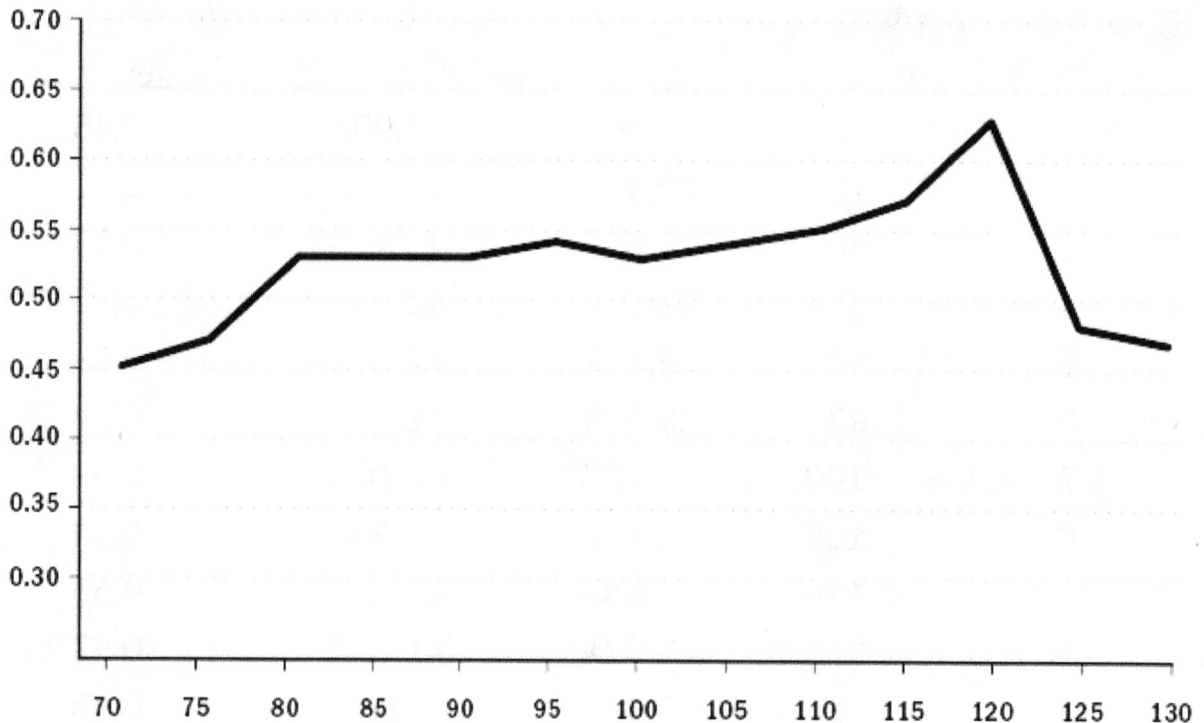

No Predictions

One of the core principles of quantitative trading, as compared to fundamental stock investing, is we are not trying to predict the future behavior of markets. We don't know what the markets will do, we just know that they will be different. Sometimes there will be bull markets, sometimes bear markets, sometimes sideways markets. There will be times when trend following works better and times when mean reversion works better.

And all of our systems are designed so that they have an edge, so that over time they attempt to make more money than they lose.

Let's say we have a long-term trend following system that makes money when the market is going up. We know it is supposed to lose money when that trend starts to bend. You've made a bunch of money, but then things dropped 20 percent and you got out. So you have a 20 percent drawdown.

If at the same time we are trading a short system that sells greed, it is losing money in the bull market. It's losing a little bit every day. When the market shifts into a downward trend, the short system starts to make money in a big way. Let's say it makes 30 percent. Now, instead of being in a 20 percent drawdown, you're up 10 percent, even as the market is dropping.

Now we can continue to trade from a position of being 10 percent up, rather than being 20 percent down and having to fight our way back to just being even. The combined systems have given us a 30 percent advantage in our combined equity curve. Combining systems smooths the equity curve, which is a record of money accumulated over time.

That's the magic of combining noncorrelated systems. The combination of systems is ten times more important than the individual parameters of a single system. Everyone wants to optimize the parameters of single systems. Many times they create a highly optimized single system that only tells them something about the past.

But if you combine them, they help each other. The key is to make sure one system is not losing too much while the other is making money.

Trading on Margin

The combined systems in this book are tested with the assumption that we can trade 100 percent long and 100 percent short simultaneously. This gives the best results, and it is an entirely reasonable approach, since the long systems tend to cover the short systems. Moreover, with careful position sizing (discussed in chapter 5), and multiple noncorrelated systems trading at once, the risks of short-trading are quite small.

Some traders—or their brokers—do not like to trade 100 percent long and short. They can trade at lesser numbers (for example, 50 percent long, 50 percent short). Their CAGR will be less but so will be their maximum drawdown, but the principles behind the systems still are sound.

In live trading, it is rare to be fully invested 100 percent long and short at the same time, even if you want to be. Many times you will not find sufficient setups to fully invest all your systems, or your trades will not be filled because of market entry parameters you have set within your setups.

Principles of Creating Systems

Make No Predictions
As I've explained, unlike fundamental traders, we don't predict what the future behavior of the market will be. Consequently, we must trade all four styles—Trend Following Long, Trend Following Short, Mean Reversion Long, Mean Reversion Short—in some form because we don't know what the future will bring.

Trade Backtested Systems
This is the only way you know you are creating an edge. Many people look at charts and say, "well, I'd get in here and get out there, and I'd make money." But they tend to see what they want to see in the charts. Nine times out of ten what they think will work doesn't actually work in real time. If you can backtest your ideas, you can save a huge amount of money because you can establish whether your idea really has an edge or not. You need to look at how your system will work in all kinds of markets. The computer will tell you if your rules actually are helping you lose money or make money.

Build Systems that Reflect Your Objectives
As I describe in chapter 4, you have to trade in a way that reflects your objectives, with a strategy that suits you. You've got to know what you want, know your risk tolerance, and stay within your comfort zone.

Limitations Trading IRAs

Financial regulations prevent trading short (stocks) in IRA accounts, and you cannot have margin accounts in IRAs. As I describe in the next chapter, trading market neutral means trading 100 percent short and 100 percent long simultaneously. Some people will just trade long in IRAs, for example, and go to cash when the market turns against a long approach. Others may choose to buy inverse ETFs in their IRAs, or use other accounts for shorting.

The Hard Part of This Approach

Let's say you build a system and backtest it. The test shows it gives a 15 percent compound annual growth rate (CAGR) and a 5 percent maximum annual drawdown. You think that looks pretty good, so you start to trade it. Here's the dangerous part: subtly, you got it in your head that you're going to get 15 percent every year. But you're not.

Maybe one year you get 30 percent. That feels fantastic. But then you get zero. Or your maximum drawdown hits 12 percent, which is outside your comfort zone. Then you get a 25 percent return the third year. Over time you may see 15 percent CAGR, but year to year the returns may be much more varied. This can be hard for some people. It can even cause people to abandon their system, although nothing is wrong with it. Always remember that it is just an average.

You could start trading a system in the first year and get zero percent return. It's a paradox, but that result does not mean there's something wrong with the system. It can simply be a reflection of the fact that results are a lot more variable than you expected. For example, if you started a long-term trend following long system coincidentally at the end of the bear market in 2009, for the next nine years you would have thought you had a great system. But if you had started it ten months earlier, straightaway you could have been into a 30 percent drawdown. You might have thought your system was deeply wrong. In fact, over time your results would smooth out and improve if you stuck with the system.

Chapter 3

Make Money in Bull, Bear and Sideways Markets

In 2008 I was trading profitably. The markets had been in a long uprun since 2003. Today, we all know that the market dropped hard that year. If I had only been trading long systems, I would have lost money. It would not have mattered what kind of long system—they all lost money. In my case I was trading both long and short.

I had seen bear markets in 2000–2002. I knew that a bear market was going to come again and that if I only traded long I would eventually lose money. I knew I needed to trade short even in a rising market, as a kind of insurance. In 2008 the S&P 500 dropped 56 percent, but because I was executing both on the long and short sides, it was a very profitable year for me. I wasn't nervous when the market went down because I didn't really care. I was positioned to take advantage of whatever the market did. I made close to 80 percent return that year.

That experience was the absolute proof that if you trade both sides of the market you do not need to worry much about market direction. Automated, noncorrelated trading absolutely worked, even when the market did very poorly. It was incredibly liberating.

In this chapter I will, using examples of four systems, show the end result of my approach and the concepts behind how we achieve that result.

Benchmarking Performance

Before we get into the performance of our systems, let's establish a benchmark. A common one is the S&P 500. Here's how it performed from January 1995 to July 2019.

Table 2: S&P 500 Performance, 1995-2019

January 2, 1995 – July 24, 2019	SPY
CAGR	8.02%
Maximum Drawdown	56.47%
Longest Drawdown	86.1 Months
Annualized Volatility	18.67%
Sharpe	0.43
MAR	0.14
Total Return	562.51%

Chart 2: S&P 500 Performance, 1995-2019 with Drawdowns

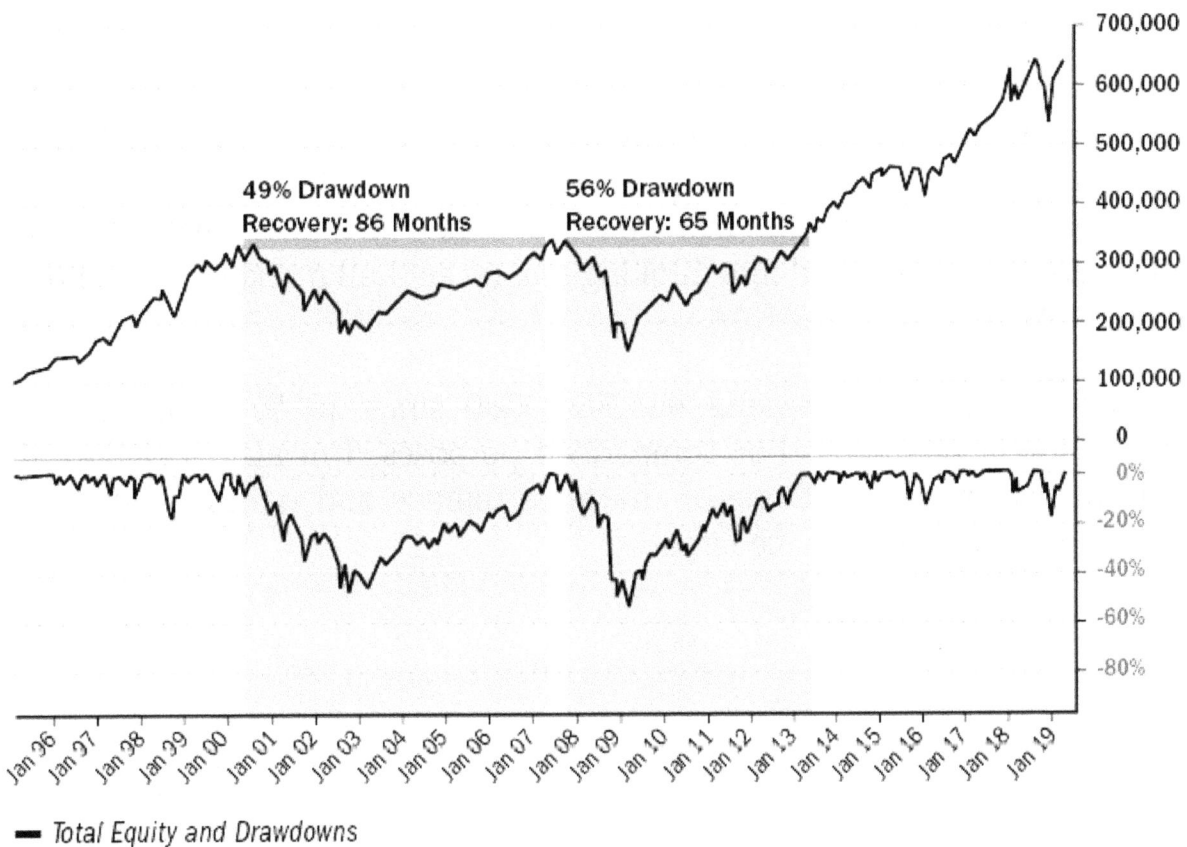

49% Drawdown
Recovery: 86 Months

56% Drawdown
Recovery: 65 Months

— Total Equity and Drawdowns

As I've already discussed, it's very important to understand that traders and markets can experience great runups—and then big drawdowns that take years to recover from.

This chart shows how we can have much larger drawdowns than expected, and it can take years to recover from them. Beginning in 1995 there was a great run-up in the market. It was a roaring bull market, and of course the bubble eventually burst. In April 2000 the S&P 500 started a drop of 49 percent that took 86 months to recover—more than seven years. The index hit new equity highs in 2007 at last—and straightaway there was another drop, this one 56 percent, and it took 65 months to recover—five-and-a-half years.

You can see that the big drop at the end of 2018 recovered very quickly. But don't let that experience, or the historic bull market run of the last decade, fool you. Someone who got in the market in 2000, if they had bought the index, would have needed thirteen years before they made money. The market experienced an 89 percent drop between 1929 and 1932—and did not reach new highs for twenty-five years.

The future will not look like the past. It will be different, and sooner or later the bears will come back in. Traders tend to forget this kind of history, especially since the last decade has been such a bull-market period. Our approach is to be prepared so that we make money no matter what the market does—and not to be lulled into thinking that recent bull markets will continue indefinitely.

The chart above, representing the S&P 500 since 1995, is our primary benchmark in this book. For comparison purposes, I'm also including the performance purposes of one of the most famous and richest men on the planet so you can see how he fared.

Table 3: Berkshire Hathaway Performance, 1996-2019

May 9, 1996 – July 24, 2019	
CAGR	9.87%
Maximum Drawdown	54.57%
Longest Drawdown	64.9 Months
Annualized Volatility	23.01%
Sharpe	0.43
MAR	0.18
Total Return	791.07%

Chart 3: Berkshire Hathaway, 1996-2019, Buy-and-Hold Performance

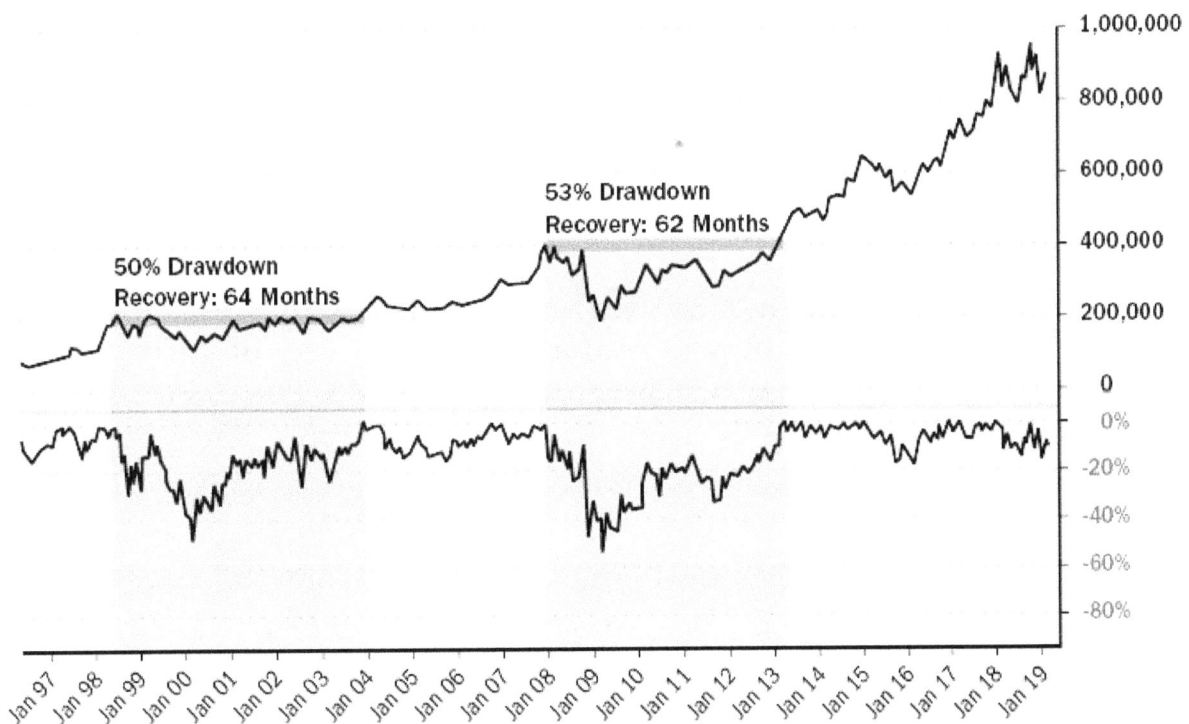

Some traders feel they can do better than the index simply by purchasing a well-run fund. Berkshire Hathaway may be the most famous conglomerate in the world. We hear that Warren Buffett is the best stock trader alive. This is probably true for him as far as net returns—but a lot of that is because he has been in the game for so long. He is enjoying the magic of compound interest. His performance is better than the S&P 500's, but he has had two drawdowns of half his principal that lasted for more than five years. If you had bought Berkshire Hathaway in the fall of 2008, straightaway you'd have a 53 percent drawdown.

Who has the stomach for that? Most people would say, "This guy has lost his touch, I'm out." Of course, it came back, but that's because Buffett has enormous patience and is willing to wait. He has a long trading strategy. Most people won't stay in the game when they lose half their money, especially for a roughly 10 percent return.

Traders like Buffett get a lot of publicity when they do well, but the negative side of their results is much less well known. As much as anything, they have a willingness to stay in the game when most traders would call it quits. The volatility of their results shows the downside of investing with a single system.

Berkshire Hathaway does not pay a dividend, so it's easy to compare to our systems. In our backtests we do not include dividends, so you can compare results on an equalized performance basis. (I like to take a conservative approach, as we do not know if dividend payments from the past will continue at the same yield).

In the following chapters you will read a step-by-step way of creating seven systems that have a combined performance as follows:

Table 4: TMS Trading System Performance vs S&P 500

January 2, 1995 – July 24, 2019	Trading System	SPY
CAGR%	30.44%	8.02%
Maximum Drawdown	11.83%	56.47%
Annualized Volatility	11.22%	18.67%
Sharpe	2.71	0.43
MAR	2.57	0.14
Total Return	68,115.39%	562.51%

Chart 4: TMS Trading System Equity Curve

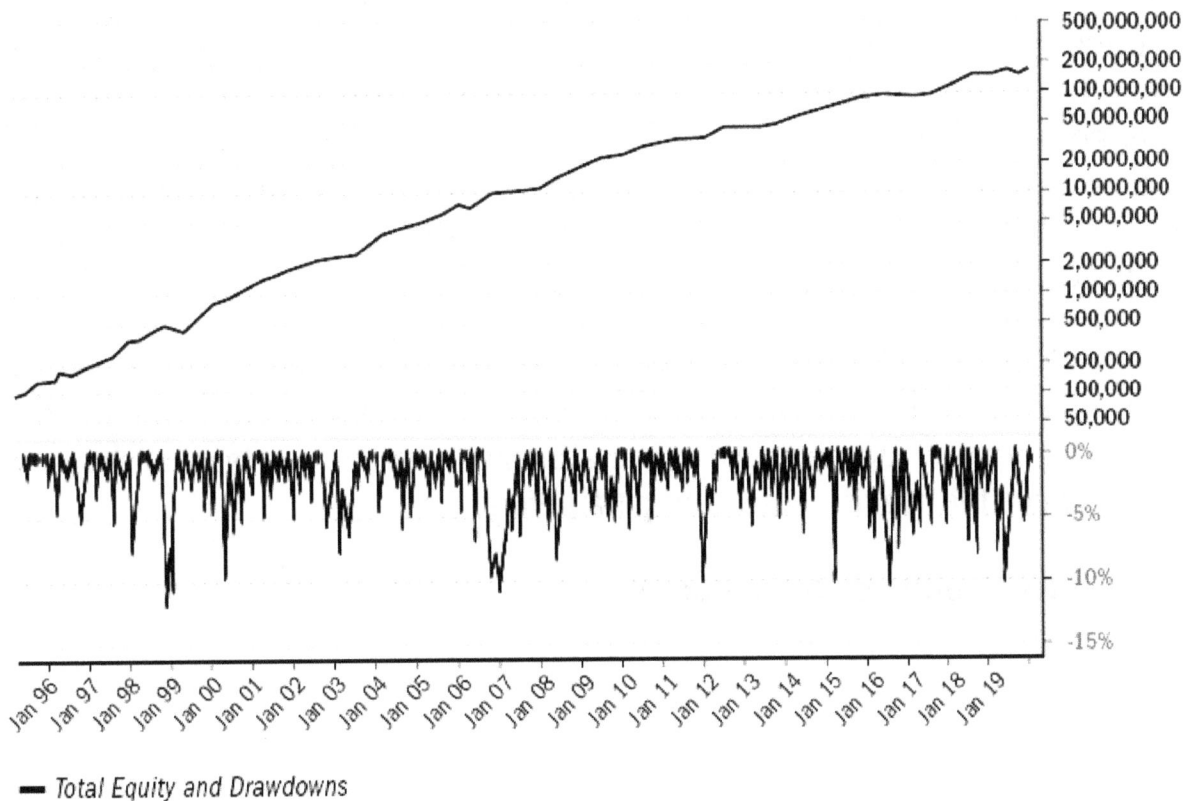

— *Total Equity and Drawdowns*

The benefits of this approach are worth enumerating, because the experience of trading this way is very different than what most traders are accustomed to:

- Substantially higher CAGR than the SPY; close to four times greater.
- Much lower drawdown; the maximum drawdown is one-fifth what the SPY experienced.
- The longest drawdown lasted only eleven months, compared to more than seven years for the SPY.
- Since 1995, the system was profitable every single year.
- Makes money in bull markets.
- Makes money in sideways markets.
- Makes money in bear markets.
- In other words, this approach is much more robust than the SPY, delivering consistent double-digit returns on backtested data, regardless of market conditions.

The Four Basic Trading Styles in Action

There are two ways to protect yourself regardless of market direction. One is to trade noncorrelated assets—classically, we are taught that stocks and bonds tend to be noncorrelated, but not always. When one goes down the other goes up, theoretically. The heart of my approach is to trade stocks, and I assume that in extreme times all stocks are correlated—so I use noncorrelated systems that take advantage of different kinds of price movements within those stocks.

Let's look at the four basic systems upon which everything in my systems is built, which I introduced in the previous chapter. In this section I am going to give you a high-level overview of the systems' approaches; later in the book I'll introduce the specific rules and parameters.

Long-Term Trend Following Long

Chart 5: REGN LTTF Long Trade

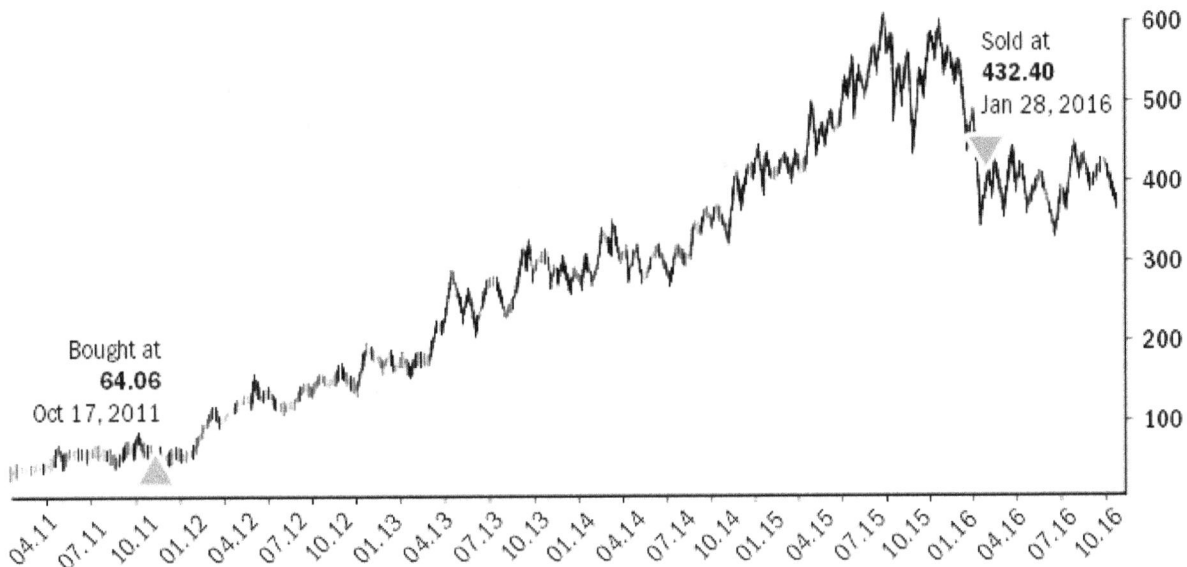

This graph illustrates a long-term trend following system that only trades long. It opens the trade when the trend is up, and its only task is to stay in the game and follow the trend as long as the market is going up and the stock is rising in price. We stay in the position until we have clear evidence that the trend is bending. Then we get out.

In this example you can see I bought the stock that this chart follows, symbol REGN, at $64.06 in 2011, and held it as it moved up to more than $600. I sold in 2016 at $432.40. You might ask, why didn't I sell it at $600? Because you never know how much higher it will go. Maybe it would have gone to $1,000. The only task of this system is to stay in until the long-term trend is clearly over, and then get out.

Obviously, systems like this can make great money in bull markets. But they lose money in sideways markets and lose or are flat in bear markets.

Chart 6: NVDA LTTF Long Trade

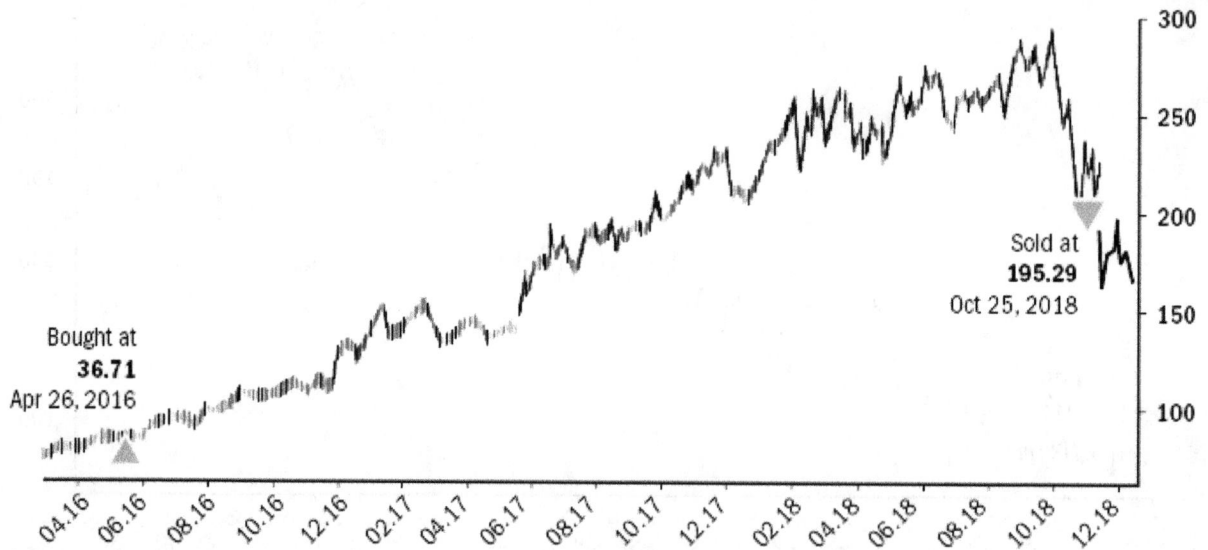

This chart, of symbol NVDA, is a perfect example of how someone would have felt trading the bull market from 2016 until it started to sell off in 2018. It shows us buying the stock at $36.71and exiting at $195.29. You'll notice that is well below the high of near $300, which is part of trading these systems. You have to give back some of your profits in order to capture the majority of the trend.

Long-Term Trend Following Short

Chart 7: SPY LTTF Short Trades

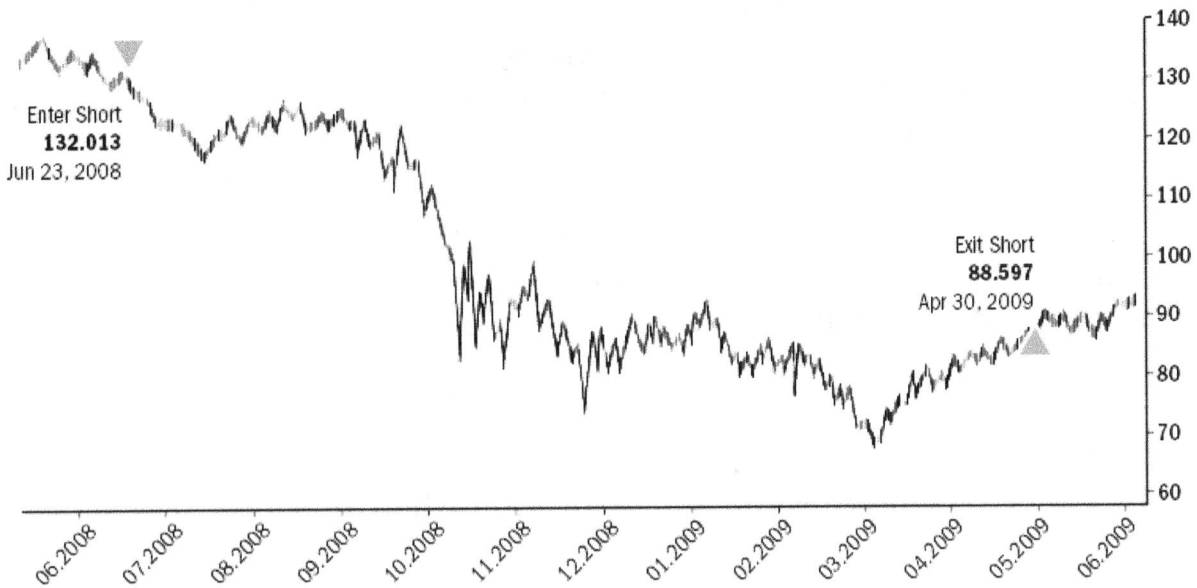

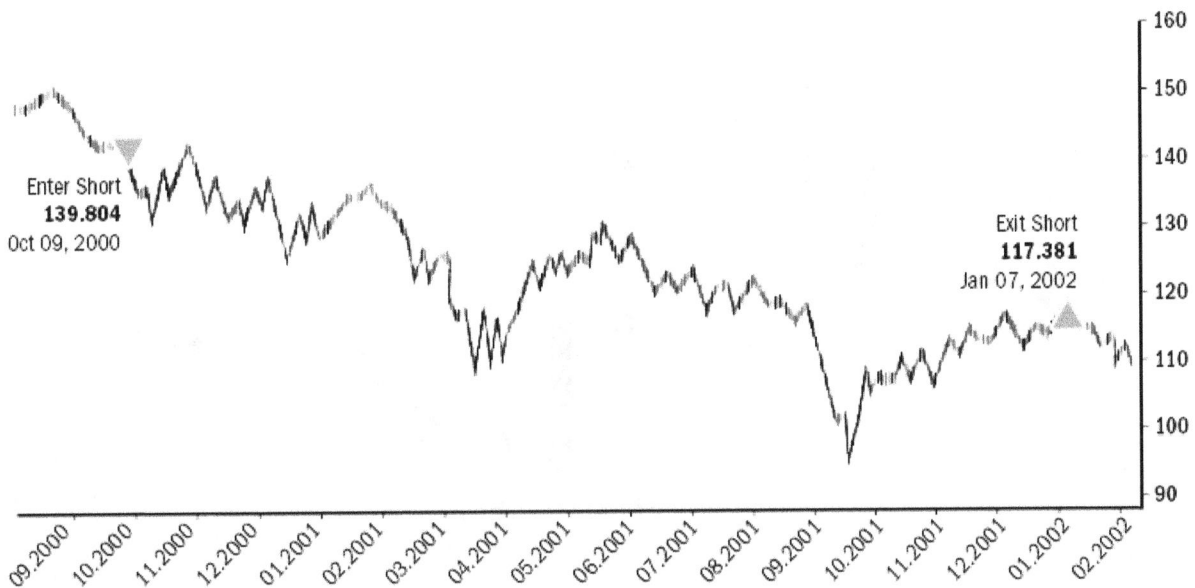

In the first chart, which begins in June of 2008, we see a clear example of how, with a simple style like trend following on the short side, you could be covered during the complete bear market in 2008. The downward trend started to establish in June and July of 2008. That triggered a trading signal and we went short on the SPY ETF at $132.01. The trade didn't do much for a few months, but we then rode it through the low point of March 2009. We captured the whole down move, making big profits on the short side, exiting at $88.59.

You might ask, why didn't I get out in March 2009, at the bottom? Because we only know it was the bottom in hindsight. The price of trend following, whether long or short, is you must be willing to give up some of your gain to ensure you capture the full run of the trend. We waited to get out until there was a clear signal that the trend was over.

The second chart shows a similar trade in the bear market of 2000–2003. We shorted the SPY when our systems saw the right setup in October 2000, at $139.80, and stayed in the trade until January 2002, exiting at $117.38. Both of these are ideal short trades in bear markets.

Mean Reversion Short

Chart 8: SGMO Mean Reversion Short Trade

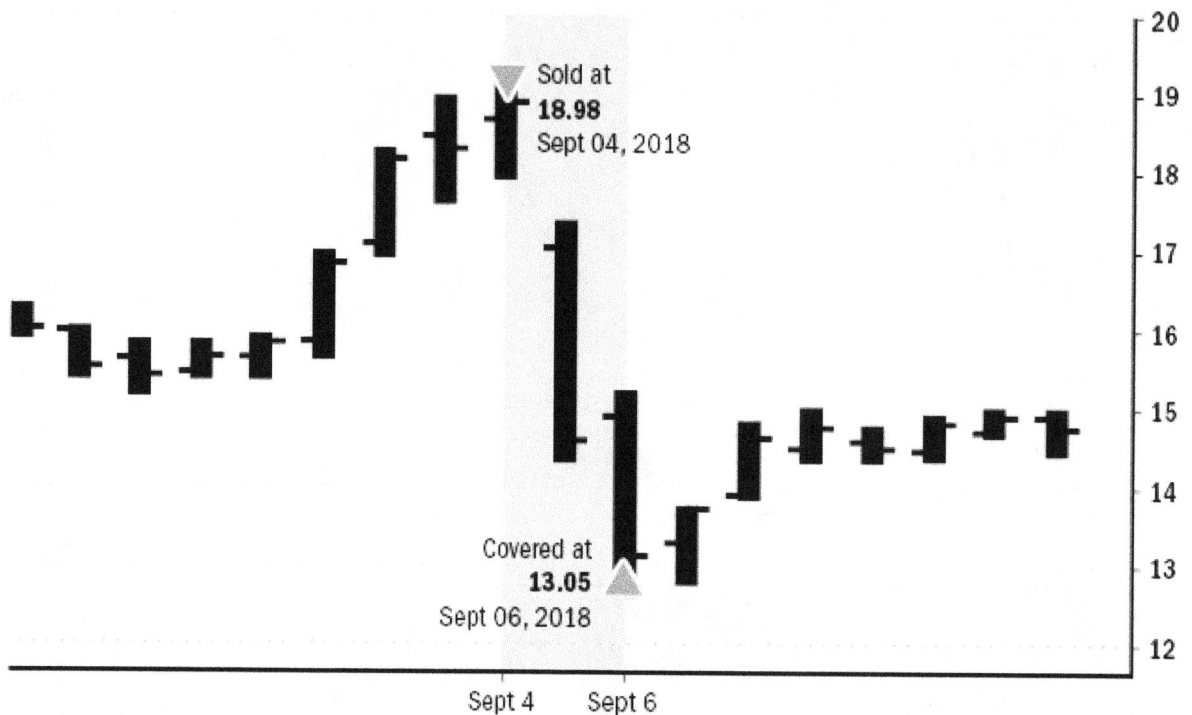

In 2018 we see a clear example of the stock SGMO, which on September 4 was so overbought that a short-selling signal triggered. This is statistically a moment when the edge is in our favor; the stock has a higher chance than random to revert back to its mean. Thus we can sell short and buy back a few days later with a profit. These trades are always short term in nature.

Chart 9: CYD Mean Reversion Short Trade

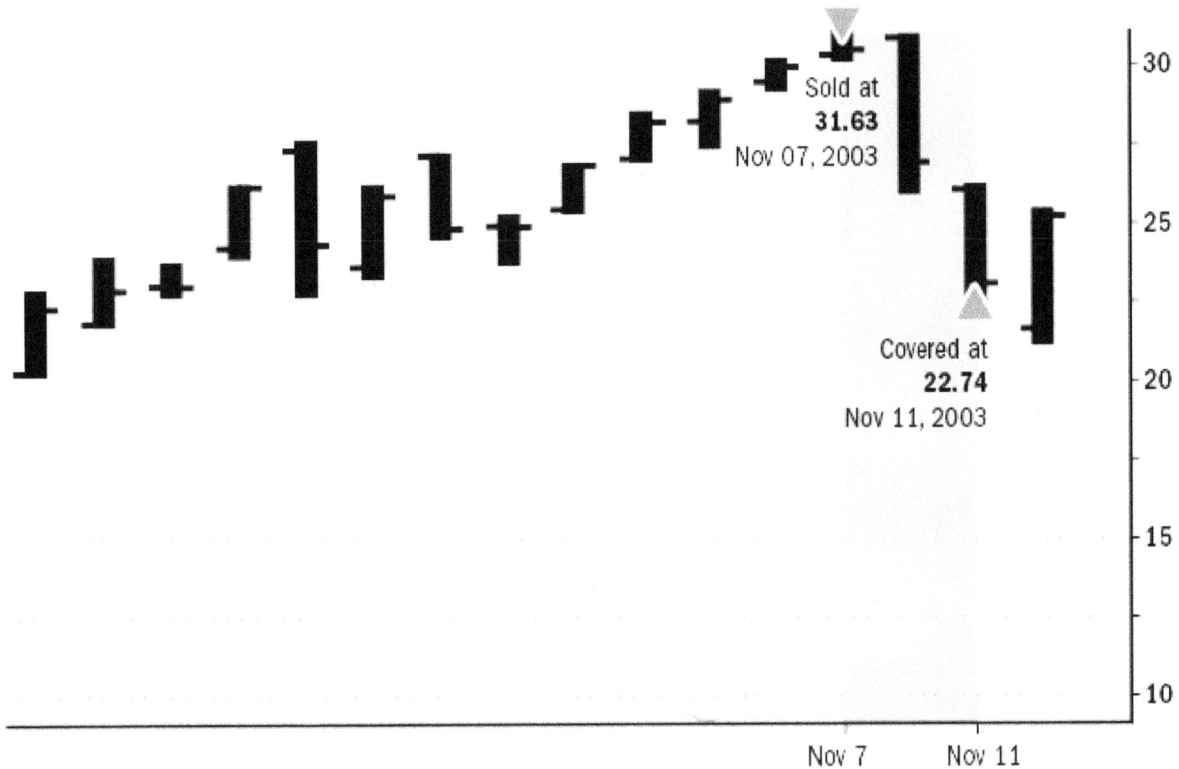

Sold at
31.63
Nov 07, 2003

Covered at
22.74
Nov 11, 2003

Nov 7   Nov 11

Another clear example with the stock CYD in November 2003. The market in this stock built up with greed, moving up from 20 to over 31 in two-weeks' time. The stock by then was so overbought that the sellers jumped in to take a profit, which drove the stock lower, and it reverted back to its mean.

As I explained above, we know we need to trade short when the market is falling, not only to make money but also to offset the money we are losing on the long side. In a mean reversion system I follow the maxim "sell greed, buy fear."

Mean Reversion Long

Chart 10: SRPT Mean Reversion Long Trade

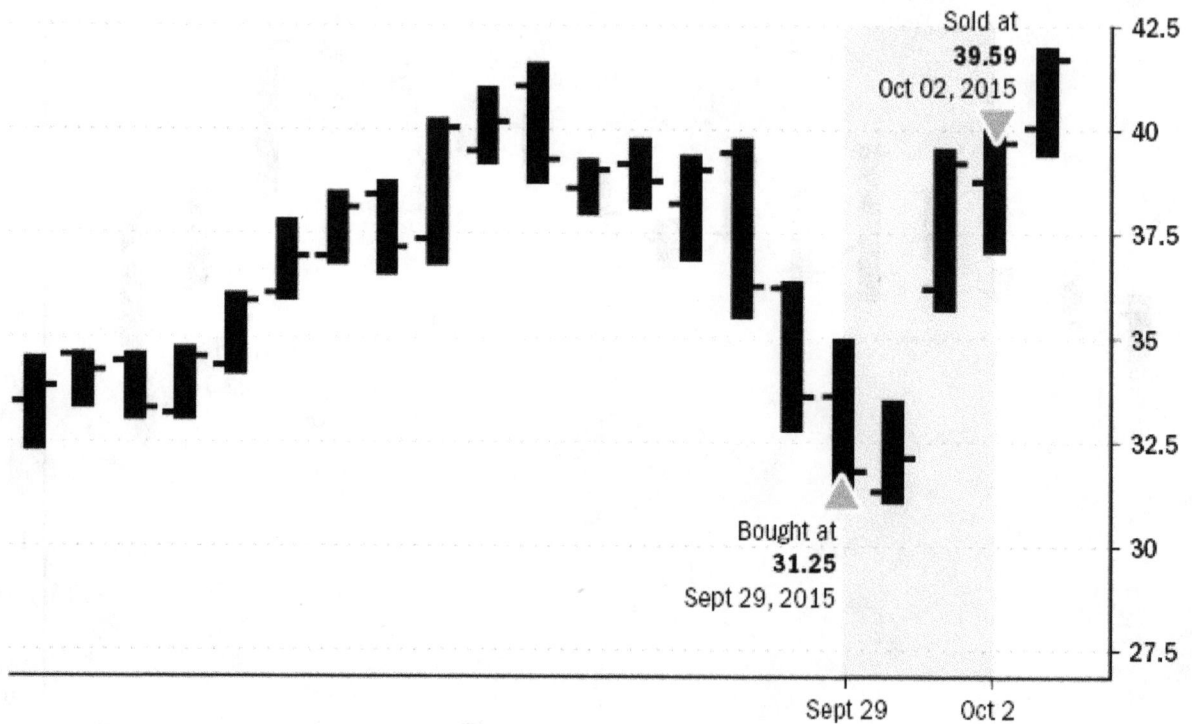

This is the other side of mean reversion. Rather than sell greed, we buy fear. We buy fear or panic and wait until a stock reverts to its mean. In this example you can see there was an uptrend and then a huge selloff. The stock was oversold. There was panic, and often this is a great time to buy a stock, because there is a statistically greater than average likelihood that the stock will return to its mean price.

I bought at $31.25 and three days later sold at $39.59.

Chart 11: GNC Mean Reversion Long Trade

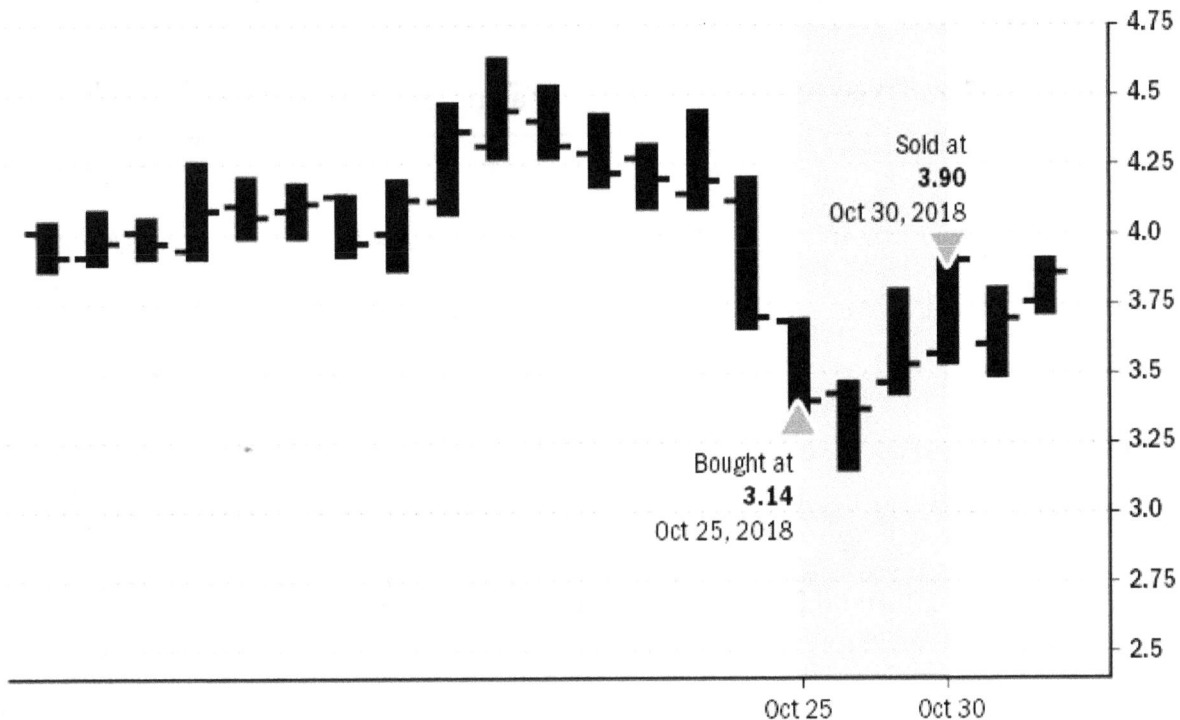

Sold at
3.90
Oct 30, 2018

Bought at
3.14
Oct 25, 2018

Oct 25   Oct 30

Here's another clear example of a great long mean reversion trade. There was a great uptrend in September and part of October in which the stock GNC moved up from 2.71 to 4.47. Then the profit taking began. This resulted in a panicked selloff. Panic is good for mean reversion long setups. The system then triggered such an oversold situation that the odds were in our favor to buy this stock. We did so at $3.14, and three trading days later we sold it back when it had reverted to its mean at $3.90.

As with mean reversion short, you only hold for a few days and then get out. You're expecting the stock to bounce back to its mean, but even if it doesn't, you still get out within a few days.

Let me be clear that these results don't happen because I'm watching these stocks carefully and have great timing. They are the product of backtested systems than employ technical indicators to signal when I should get in and get out. This is a core concept of my approach.

Results: Combing Noncorrelated Systems, Different Styles

and Different Directions

Table 5: Long Term Trend Following Long Single-System Performance

January 2, 1995 – July 24, 2019	Trading System	SPY
CAGR%	22.52%	8.02%
Maximum Drawdown	42.14%	56.47%
Annualized Volatility	22.70%	18.67%
Sharpe	0.99	0.43
MAR	0.53	0.14
Total Return	14,560.64%	562.51%

Chart 12: Trend Following Long Single-System Performance

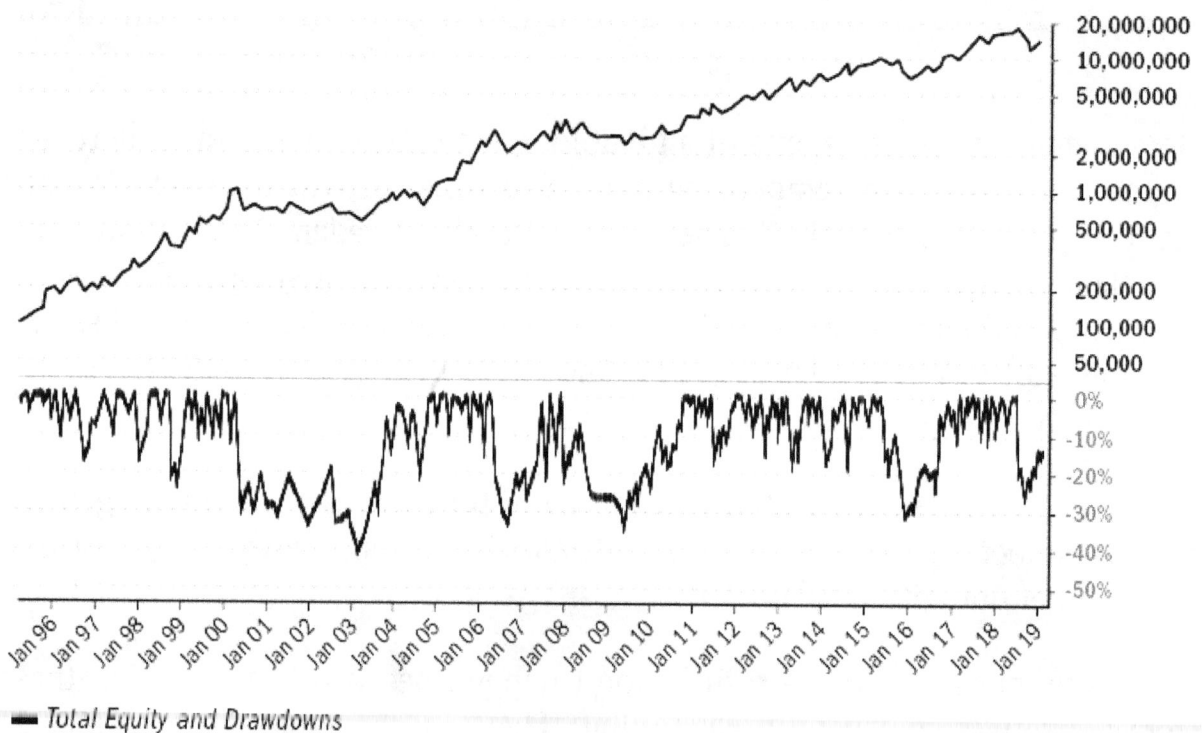

■ Total Equity and Drawdowns

The graphics in this section, like those throughout the book that show the performance of systems, represent backtested results from 1995 to 2019. Since 1995, this long-term trend following system had a compounded annual growth rate (CAGR) of a little bit more than 22 percent. The maximum drawdown was 42 percent, which is way too large for most people to handle. The longest drawdown lasted four-and-a-half years. They can't stand to lose that much of their equity and keep trading. Everybody would be happy to achieve 22 percent average return over the last twenty-four years, which is way better than the S&P 500 index benchmark of about 8 percent. But if they experience those drawdowns, losing close to half of their money, they'll run away.

Table 6: Mean Reversion Short Single-System Performance

January 2, 1995 – July 24, 2019	Trading System	SPY
CAGR%	18.14%	8.02%
Maximum Drawdown	24.66%	56.47%
Annualized Volatility	11.50%	18.67%
Sharpe	1.58	0.43
MAR	0.74	0.14
Total Return	5,897.58%	562.51%

Chart 13: Mean Reversion Short Single-System Performance

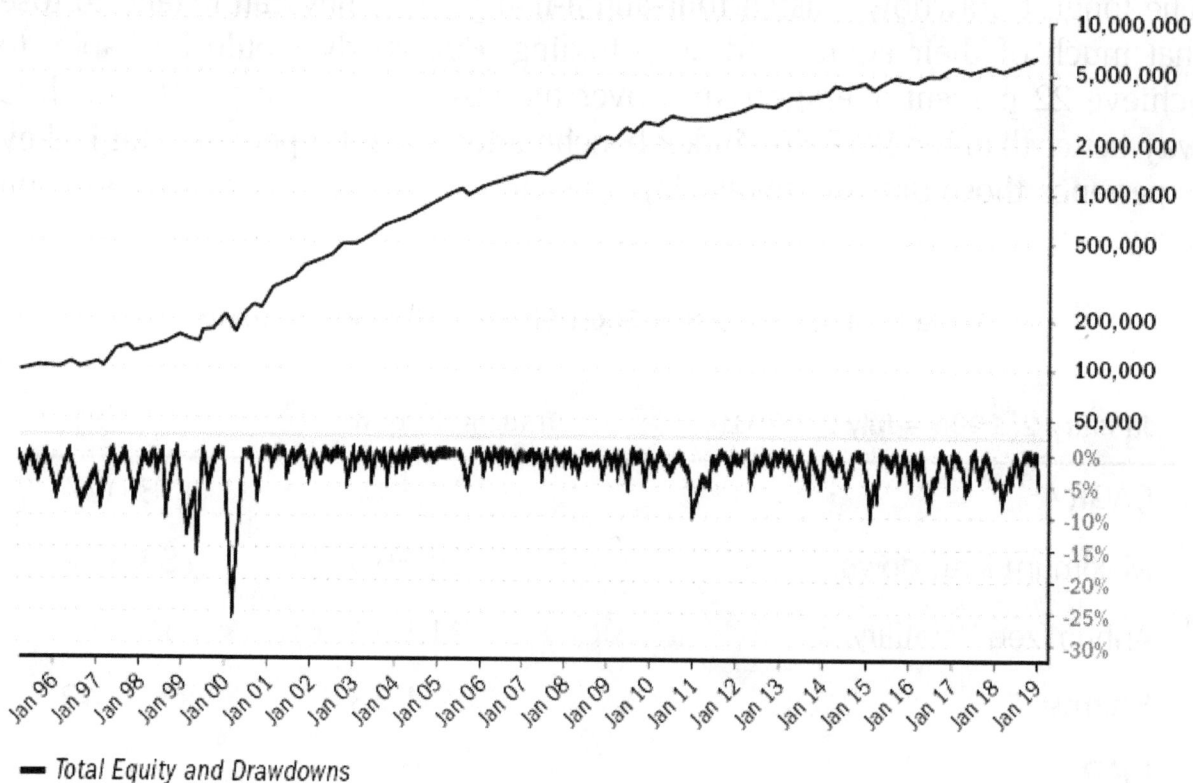

— *Total Equity and Drawdowns*

The mean reversion short system had a decent return over the same time period of 18 percent, and a maximum drawdown of 24 percent.

The Magic of Combining Different Systems with Different Directions and Different Styles

Long Trend Following and Short Mean Reversion

But look what happens when you combine both of these systems, which I do by trading 100 percent long and 100 percent short at the same time. You can do this with a margin account, and when I am fully invested long and short at the same time I consider my positions to be flat, because each side covers the other side.

When the two systems are traded in combination this way, both trends improve. The CAGR comes up to 43 percent, and the maximum drawdown drops to 31 percent. Moreover, the longest drawdown is now only sixteen months, during a period when the S&P 500 was in drawdown for eighty months, from 2003 to 2007. It took that long for the market to get back to its previous highs. The MAR improved to 1.37.

Performance of the two systems combined:

Table 7: Combined Performance, Long Term Trend Following Long and Mean Reversion Short Systems

January 2, 1995 – July 24, 2019	Trading System	SPY
CAGR%	43.13%	8.02%
Maximum Drawdown	31.54%	56.47%
Annualized Volatility	20.70%	18.67%
Sharpe	2.08	0.43
MAR	1.37	0.14
Total Return	666,623.64%	562.51%

Chart 14: Combined Performance, Long Term Trend Following Long and Mean Reversion Short Systems

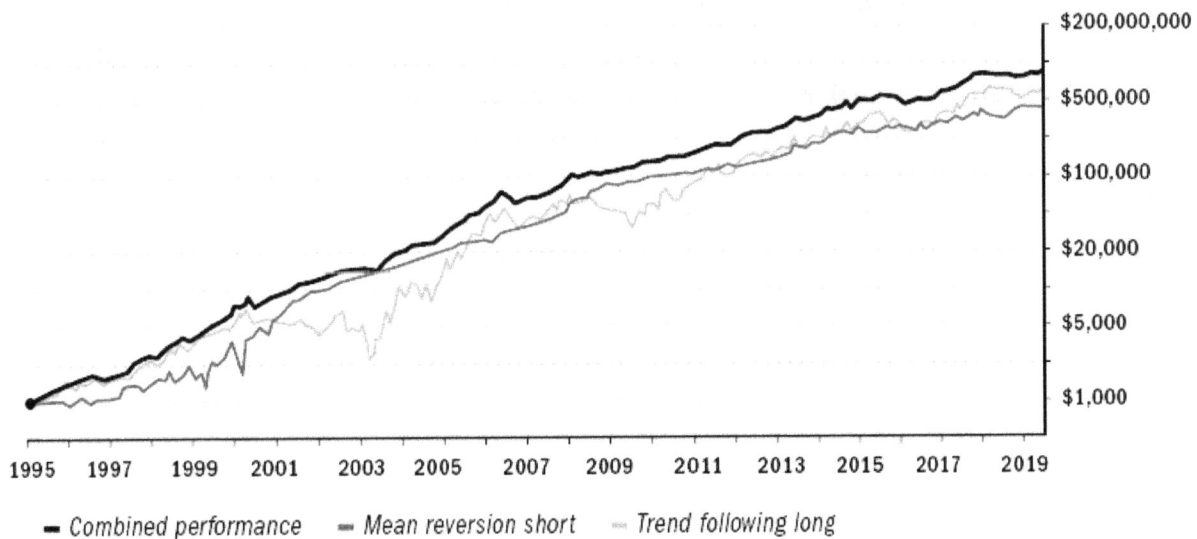

— Combined performance   — Mean reversion short   — Trend following long

You might think that the two systems are a zero-sum game, that they cancel each other out. But they don't. With the long system we try to capitalize as much as possible when the trends are in our favor, and then minimize losses when they're not. Looking at the equity chart above, you can see the long system made money in favorable times when the markets went up and then went to cash because there were no opportunities, or set-ups, to trade (such as 2008). At the same time the short system's accumulated equity was making money when the market was going down.

If you know you can make money not only when the market is rising but also in a down market like 2000, 2008, or late 2018, you will be very comfortable trading systems like these. You'll know your system has no real preference for what the market will actually do. The only thing necessary is for there to be movement in the markets. Even if that movement is sideways, shorter term systems like mean reversion short and mean reversion long can produce profits. Stocks will move in a band, and a mean reversion system will short overbought stocks and buy oversold stocks, waiting for them to snap back to their mean.

These are the basic structures of trading noncorrelated trading: combine different directions and different styles, that is, trade long and short and trade trend following and mean reversion.

You may be eager to see all the rules of all systems right away. But before we get into the mechanics of system creation, including the 12 secret ingredients of every system, you need to step back and ask yourself some fundamental questions. That's what the next chapter is about.

Chapter 4

To Succeed, First Define Your Objectives

Why do we need objectives? After all, there is a universal trading objective. When I ask anyone who wants to invest what their objective is, the first answer they all give is, "I want to make as much money as possible with the lowest risk possible." That's what everybody wants.

In fact, that answer doesn't make any sense at all, as I'll explain in a moment.

The second answer I hear is that they want to trade like me or some famous trader or hedge fund manager. "I just want to learn from the best," they say, "and do the same."

Why should they reinvent the wheel? I'll tell you why: because it is simply not possible to "do the same." My personal situation, my preferences, my strengths and weaknesses are all different from anyone else's. For example, consider beliefs. If someone believes the market will go up forever, they have a very strong bull bias, and they can trade that way. If someone else lives in an environment where there is a high tax on trading profits, they will develop different beliefs about how they can invest. Warren Buffett, for example, doesn't do shorter-term trades because he doesn't like the higher tax rate he has to pay on those gains and doesn't believe in shorter-term systems in general. On the other hand, there are many famous traders who rely only on short-term systems and do not believe in the slow-moving, longer-term approach. Bottom line: there are systems for everybody.

Then there's volatility. Some people are comfortable with high-volatility stocks like Tesla and Netflix. Others want very stable stocks, such as those found in the S&P 100. Those levels of comfort or discomfort drive them toward certain trading systems.

Others can't stand closing a trade without a profit—a belief that may derive from what they learned in grade school, that a "C" is a bad grade, it represents failure, and they can't handle it. Or there are people who say, "you will never go broke taking profits." (That's actually not true. If they continually take small profits, one day they will get a big loser that keeps dropping, and they won't be able psychologically to close the trade out and take the loss. Their loss aversion will actually worsen the loss.)

Another belief system says that risk is fine. These people will say, I want to risk a small amount of money, I don't care if I lose it. Like one of the greatest traders ever, Paul Tudor Jones, they'll look for asymmetrical returns in which the average winning trade is much greater than the average losing trade. This approach means that you might lose 60 or 70 percent of the time or more. Even though, over time, they make money, this loss rate is just too much psychologically for many people to handle.

These sorts of differences in outlook and risk tolerance quickly push people toward different trading systems. Let's consider four examples of different situations that lead to different approaches.

John

John is twenty-eight years old, he lives a high-paced life, and he's very impatient. He has a $30,000 trading account and he's a bit of a gambler. He is very aggressive as a trader, but he's young, he's highly paid at his job, and so he doesn't care too much if his account drops 35 percent. He doesn't have any kids and he's not thinking about retirement. He likes the excitement of trading, is happy to do it every day on his computer, and if he makes more money he'll use it to buy a nicer car.

Jim

Jim, on the other hand, is fifty-five years old. He's still working but he'd like to retire. He has $2 million in his accounts and a lot less risk tolerance than John. He has worked a long time to accumulate that money and he doesn't want to lose it. He wants it to grow at a nice, steady pace, and he can't imagine losing more than 15 percent because that would jeopardize his retirement. He's comfortable around computers but he doesn't want to be glued to one to do his trading. If he can compound his money at around 15 percent per year with low risk and low volatility, he will be very comfortable.

Donald

Donald, our third trader, is seventy-two years old and has $7 million, mostly in IRA accounts. He hates to pay taxes and prefers a buy-and-hold strategy. The world of computers largely passed him by, so while he can use one, he's not very comfortable with them.

Brian

Brian, forty-six years old, is a well-paid executive who has a very busy life. He's got $500,000 in his trading account, he's good with math and computers, and he wants to accumulate more wealth, but he doesn't have a lot of time. He can find an hour a week, at most, to trade.

Every one of these individuals can trade in the markets, but for each to succeed they would need a different trading approach that reflected who they are psychologically, where they are professionally, where they are in life, and more. None of them would benefit from trying to clone my approach, because it would not reflect them, and consequently they would not be able to stick to it. For them to trade successfully, they have to be 100 percent clear about themselves and their objectives.

Someone who wants to trade needs to ask themselves questions like these:

- What is your level of comfort doing technical analysis?
- How good are you with math?
- How are your computer skills?
- Are you a detail person, or more oriented toward the big picture?
- Do you like working with numbers?
- Are you analytical or not?
- Is the account taxable or not?
- How much time do you have each day to execute your systems?

The time question is one some people may not think about. Some people are happy to be glued to the screen. Some want to do half an hour a day, or they lead busy lives with kids and jobs and can only trade weekly or monthly. Some want to trade accounts for themselves and accounts for their kids, others want to keep it super simple. They may have a $5 million account, or a $5,000 account. With a $5 million account, you have many more opportunities to build many noncorrelated systems. With a $5,000 account, it's better to keep it simple.

Whatever your answers to these questions, there is a strategy for you.

Perhaps the most important thing I like to ask people is, "what does your perfect life as a trader look like?" That can reveal a lot. From there we go into objectives, which I divide between *overall objectives* and individual *system objectives*.

Overall Objectives

Personal Objectives

This means answering questions around how you would define your perfect life as a trader, looking at your personal situation and asking what you really want.

What is your reason for trading? Is it for wealth accumulation? Monthly cash flow? Or do you have some other objective? Many people have less obvious objectives that can actually be bad for their trading success. For example, they may want to be in a high-paced environment. They may live a boring life and want some excitement. They have a boring job, they see traders who seem to have very exciting lives, and they want that. They may crave the high of winning at a game. These approaches can be very dangerous. They will take position sizes that are too large, and if the market turns against them it can wipe out their trading account. This is not a game: these are your finances, and your motivations for how you handle them need to be well understood and managed.

Psychological Objectives

How do you want to feel during trading? The answer will be different for everybody, but it should be defined, because you need to determine the mental state that guarantees you do not override your systems. There can be no second-guessing, no hesitation or doubt about your positions, no fear, no insecurity—nor too much excitement, either. (If you're too excited, that means you're making too much profit, which means you're taking too much risk.) When you're risking too much, when the market turns down, that excitement turns into fear. You need a mental state that guarantees flawless trading. One of the beliefs of top traders is that trading should be kind of boring. If you approach it as boring, then you can execute your trading systems because you are not emotionally attached to any trade.

Risk Tolerance Objectives

What is the average drawdown you can handle easily in live trading? Without exception, every single trader I know overestimates this number. They'll look at an equity curve that goes up from left to right, and that's the part they see. They don't focus on the 20 percent drawdown. They say, "sure, it draws down, but it's making money." Experience has taught me that 99 percent of all traders should cut their acceptable drawdown estimate in half, because otherwise they'll chicken out when they get close to those numbers.

There's another question: What is the maximum drawdown you can handle in live trading without suspending the system? The average drawdown is something you just need to deal with, because you're risking money to make money. At times your system will be hit harder than normal, and that's when you may be due for an upward move. But if the maximum drawdown is larger than you expected, that's also when most people suspend and throw in the towel. You need to be able to trade within these drawdowns without any second thoughts that could lead you to suspend trading the system.

Then there is the question of the duration of the drawdown. How long can you tolerate being underwater and not making money? As we've already seen, after the 2000–2003 bear market it was seven years before the S&P 500 got back to where it had been and began making money. Generally, with our systems those durations are much shorter, but if you can't handle a long drawdown duration you need a system with a high trade frequency. For example, if your system only trades ten times per year and you have a 20 percent drawdown, you stay there for a long time because it's quite possible that no trades are generated. A higher trade frequency will find opportunities sooner and get you out sooner.

Return and Profit Objectives

This is where everybody wants to start! They want to make 100 percent return per year, but they have to see that the return objectives are in line with the risk objectives. They look at that exciting profit objective, but they don't understand that if they want to make 100 percent per year they are going to have to risk the bank. Return and risk are always in line. If you want a high return, you must be able to handle a high risk.

I have people who say, "Okay, I get that. I want at least 30 or 40 percent return, but I can't handle more than a 4 percent drop in my accounts." I tell them they simply can't achieve that in the long term. They might achieve it in an over-optimized backtest, but they're going to exceed that drawdown in live trading and then chicken out.

The more you are willing and psychologically able to risk, the higher your returns can be if your system has a significant edge. But the risk has to be in line with what you are comfortable with. You have to understand that you need those drawdowns because you are risking money. If you're not able to risk money, just go to cash and get zero percent.

Style Objectives

There are basically two styles, as I've previously shown: trend following, and mean reversion or counter-trend. In the trend-following style, we follow trends, preferably of long duration, sticking with it until the trend bends. The longer the trend duration, the better the profits. It's a very boring system for many people because there's not that much activity. Boring is the objective.

The issue with trend following, as I mentioned above, is you have to withstand some pretty large drawdowns, and it only makes money 30 or 40 percent of the time, when the markets are actually trending. Otherwise the markets are sideways. Most of the times the trend following systems don't do that well until there is a trend, and then they make big money.

The mean reversion style is generally a short-duration trading style. For example, you buy a stock that has been oversold with the expectation that it will revert to its statistical mean. The statistical likelihood of a move in that direction is in your favor; that's your edge. You hold positions only for a few days, and the expected profit on each trade is quite small. That means you must have a high trade frequency to make big returns. If you traded only twenty times per year, you might have a high win rate of 70 percent, but your CAGR could be only 1 percent for the year. You might enter a trade at 10 and sell at 11. That's good, but you need to do that many times to pile up a good return. On the other hand, you could enter a single trade in a trend-following system and have theoretically unlimited return, so long as the trend continued.

Someone who is impatient probably will prefer mean reversion, because there's a higher win rate and more action. Other people prefer the quiet approach of trend following.

The best of both worlds—and the heart of what this book is about—is when you combine both styles you can exponentially increase your CAGR while reducing your drawdowns.

Directional Objectives

We can trade both long and short, as I've described. Long trading is speculating on an upward moving market, short trading on a down market. We know from our backtest data sample that the market clearly has a long bias; that is, it has risen 8 percent per year, on average, over the last twenty-four years.

If you are trading inside an IRA account, your directional objectives are limited by regulations that don't allow short-selling of stocks in those accounts. I also know traders who don't like to short because they feel it is unpatriotic to bet on a company's stock moving down. That doesn't bother me, but if that's a value you have, that's fine.

More broadly, some people are uncomfortable with shorting because the risk of loss is theoretically unlimited. Here's what I mean:

Let's say you enter a long trade of 1,000 shares in a stock at $10, and the next day the stock opens at zero. You have lost your entire investment of $10,000.

Now let's say that instead of buying long, you shorted 1,000 shares of that stock at $10. You are betting the stock will drop from $10 to $8, and you'll make the difference—$2,000. Instead, it opens tomorrow at $30. You have to cover your position. You're not out $2,000, you're out $20,000. If it opens at $50, even worse: you're out $40,000. This level of risk is unacceptable to many people. It doesn't matter if you have a stop-loss in the market.

Timeframe Objectives

What kind of trades do you want to have? Do you want to grab fast profits? Do you want to engage in day trading where you have no overnight risk because you close out all your positions at the end of every day? Many people want to sleep well knowing they have no overnight market exposure. If you are worried about your positions after the close of the market or during the weekend, then overnight trading might not be for you. You may prefer day trading.

Or do you say, "I like long-term positions because I think there's too much noise in the markets. I think I need to give the market room to move and be more patient."

As with the style and directional objectives, if you are comfortable combining short and long time frames, you will improve your results.

Operational Objectives

How do you want to trade? Specifically, when do you want to enter your trades? Do you only enter them once, before the market opens, and then don't look at them after that? Do you want to watch them carefully and be glued to the screen the whole day? Do you want to enter them manually or use an automated platform? There are many options that will influence your day-to-day operations and thus the trading systems you design.

Single System Objectives

With the overall objectives established, let's turn our attention to the single-system objectives. Our strategy is made up of multiple, noncorrelated systems. For each system we ask a series of questions.

First, how does the system fit into the overall strategy? That is, when does it need to make money, and when is it supposed to lose money? The second question can make some people very uncomfortable, because they have a tendency to want to develop a single system that makes money every month.

Noncorrelated systems, by their very definition, will lose money when other systems are making money. Using a lot of computing power we can actually design systems like that, but they will be overoptimized—that is, they will be designed to fit the past, but won't do nearly as well in the future because the future does not mirror the past.

Here's an example of how a system is supposed to lose money. Let's say you devise a long-term trend following system that rides rising trends in bull markets. You do your analysis and see that it makes big money from 2013 to 2017, but there are times in the backtest when it loses money, like the bear market of 2008 and the end of 2018. You can't expect a system built this way to make money when the market drops 56 percent. That is a totally unrealistic expectation, and you must have clarity around that. Also, don't imagine that you will be able to develop special systems that always select great stocks and thus always make money and can escape strong downward moves in the market. Big downtrends mean a lot of panic. There is so much selling pressure that most stocks become 100 percent correlated with the larger market, regardless of sector or industry.

Second, what portfolio do you want to trade and why? Do you want a large portfolio with a lot of stocks so you can get a high trade frequency, or do you want a small portfolio with only index constituents from the S&P 500 for trend following because it has an upward bias and contains stocks from more liquid companies that are generally assumed to be safer? Do you want high-volume or low-volume stocks? For instance, if you select low volume, you will not participate with institutional traders. You're in a completely different arena. Does that seem like an advantage or a disadvantage?

What kind of price filters do you want? As with volume, if you choose to trade very low-priced stocks you will be out of the arena the big institutions trade in. They invest billions of dollars and can't be involved in markets where their investments move prices. Below $10, you generally won't see big institutions involved. Some people like trading penny stocks, which have huge volatility. Or maybe you prefer boring, large-cap stocks of mature companies.

When are you going to feel comfortable entering a trade? For instance, some people like to look at the overall market and only enter a trade when the S&P

500 is in an upward trend.

How do you want to enter the trade? Market on open, or a limit order? Can you accept some slippage in order to be sure you get into the trade, or do you want to enter only on a predetermined price? A guaranteed trade execution is obtained with a "market on open" order. This sometimes means that you will have some slippage.

Similarly, what is your indicator for getting out of the trade? Before you get into a trade you must know how you are going to get out of it.

What is your stop-loss? This relates to how you define and limit your risk. You must know exactly what you are willing to lose. This initial stop-loss defines your trade frequency. If you have a very small initial stop, there is a high likelihood you will be stopped out. If you have a wide stop, there is less chance of immediately getting stopped out. Also this generally gives a lower trade frequency. At the same time, it generally defines the win rate: what percentage of your trades will end up as winners. A small stop seems like it saves you from losing principal, but you can end up being whipsawed: you'll get stopped out at a small loss, only to see the stock rise because your small stop was inside the volatility of range.

What about your trailing stop-loss on a trend following system? This is a reflection of how much profit you are willing to give back. If you are very greedy, you may have a small trailing stop-loss because you don't want to give back much profit in a pullback. But you may be stopped out as part of a minor correction on a larger trend, missing out on even more profit.

When do you want to take profits? Trend followers just follow the trend until it bends and the trailing stop takes them out. Shorter term traders like profit targets. They say, "I got in at $10, if in three days it goes to $11 I want to get out." If you have a very small profit target where you get out immediately, then you will have a high percentage of winning trades.

When do you want to exit? During the day, at market on close, at market on open.

Once we know the answers to these questions, they become the parameters by which we design a system. You set up the system, backtest, and try to optimize to see what results you get.

Conceptually Correct Systems

In today's world we have access to unprecedented computing power. We can backtest many, many different parameters. Certain software providers even have an "optimize" button that looks at all the parameters and tells you, "if you did this, and this, and this, you would have the best results." Some people think that is a great way to develop a trading system, but really it's just data mining. It will tell you how to set the parameters to take advantage of everything that happened in the past—but the future will always be different, and your results will be, too—potentially *very* different.

On the other hand, if you wish to develop a conceptually correct system you will start with a premise, such as "I know a long-term trend following long system will make money when the market goes up, and I expect it to lose money when the market goes down." Or let's say you want to develop a long-term trend following short system. You know that most years it is going to lose money as the market rises. Every year, it loses a few percent. But when a big crisis comes, like the collapse of 2008, you know you're going to make big money. You're taking those losses as an insurance policy.

Compared to mining data to get the "perfect" system, look for concepts that you know will work in certain situations. You define simple rules that measure price action in certain markets and apply a conceptually correct idea of when to enter and exit.

If then we combine multiple correct concepts, it gets as close as possible to the Holy Grail.

Why Traders Fail

I asked a colleague how his trading was going, and he told me he had suspended it. He had experienced a 10 percent drawdown, and it made him feel very uncomfortable—even though he had told me he would be comfortable with that. He hadn't really understood himself.

Many people have a tendency to focus on the returns. They see the possibility of 40 percent or 50 percent CAGR, they put that into their spreadsheets and calculate how much money they can have in ten or twenty years and be dreaming about a bigger house or a boat. They focus on the returns and forget about the drawdowns. Then, when drawdowns happen they realize they can't handle them.

When I start working with clients, they want to get into the software right away and start building systems. Instead, I spend the first month with them on their psychology and their objectives. If they skip over that part, they are not going to trade their systems effectively, because they won't have built systems that truly reflect their beliefs, their lifestyles, and their preferences. The key to successful trading is to stay in the game, and traders who have not done this deep work ahead of time are less likely to do so.

Those whom I have seen fail do so because they overestimate the risk they can handle. I ask them about their risk objectives—maximum drawdown, average drawdown, and drawdown duration that they feel they can comfortably handle—and they give me an answer. Let's say a trader has $500,000 and he tells me he can comfortably handle a 30 percent drawdown. He has worked twenty years to accumulate this money. I ask him, "After a year, you have $350,000. How do you feel?" Nine out of ten say, "Terrible!" I ask if he still felt he would be able to trade in that state of mind. Many of them cannot.

Such a drawdown, or greater, absolutely is possible. You can have a drawdown, and then there's no reason it can't happen again and again. Most traders don't think that way, especially after the bull market we've had for a decade. But it can happen. The bear market of the Great Depression ended in 1933, but it was twenty-five years before the market was back to break-even. Twenty-five years of drawdown. How would you feel about that?

The systems I build, and you can build, can have much less drawdown than that, but you need to be comfortable living in drawdown. You need to think through fully how that will feel.

I tell all my clients to start slow. Settle for a 15 percent annual return instead of 30 percent. See if you can handle the daily fluctuations in your accounts. See if you can handle a couple of large drawdowns. If you can, then increase your risk a little bit. But do it slowly, because if you suspend trading you will do it at the worst possible moment, when things are down and your decision is based not on rational analysis but a poor emotional state.

Chapter 5

Using Position Sizing to Achieve Your Financial Goals

Position sizing is the most powerful lever for managing risk and achieving your objectives in trading.

We calculate the right positing sizing by taking into account the financial objectives of the trader, and, as I've explained, every trader is different. Every trader has a different risk tolerance and profit objective. Some are conservative, some can handle larger drawdowns and so on.

Every system has a buy and sell engine—a set of rules that you create. Yet through position sizing we can completely change the returns. For example, if we have a low-risk position sizing strategy, the growth rate will be a lot lower, but so will the drawdown.

If someone wants to be a lot more aggressive and shoot for the moon, they can do so with a different position sizing strategy yet use the same buy and sell decisions, just with different sizing.

Here you see two totally different results based on a different position sizing strategy although the buy and sell decisions were exactly the same.

Table 8: Effect of Position Sizing on Results

	Ending Balance	CAGR%	Max Total Equity DD	MAR
Very conservative sizing	3,166,436.78	15.11%	25.30%	0.6
Aggressive sizing	72,555,715.52	30.77%	56.10%	0.55

After I explain how we size our positions, I'll show you more examples. Let's understand position sizing first.

If you size your positions incorrectly for your own objectives and risk tolerance, you won't notice that you have done this at first, so long as you are making money. It's only when you start to lose money that you realize your mistake. For example, let's say a trader buys a position at $30, and overnight it drops to $15. He's lost 50 percent of his position. His position sizing rules for equity allocation determine how much of his total equity he has lost. Too-aggressive position sizing can make your stomach hurt. If his position sizing of this particular stock was 10 percent of his account, he just lost 5 percent of his total equity. If it was 5 percent, he lost 2.5 percent.

If he hasn't thought that scenario through carefully ahead of time, he's now facing a larger drawdown than he can stomach. All of a sudden, he's feeling a lot of discomfort. That discomfort makes it harder for him to trade his system consistently. He may start to doubt his trades because he thinks the buy-sell rules are incorrect, and fear gets involved. But the problem causing his fear is not the buy-sell rules, it's that his position sizing was wrong and exposed him to more risk than he was willing to take.

Most traders, when they think this through correctly, set more conservative position sizes. They accept a lower CAGR in exchange for a more comfortable predicted drawdown.

Position Sizing Approaches

For each system we look at the past for volatility but also make sure that we are aware that future volatility can and most likely will be different, so we size in two ways:

- Percent size: Allocate a percentage of total equity to a given trade. This is simpler—for example, if you are trading a maximum of ten positions, you allocate 10 percent of your equity to each position. Although simpler, it doesn't consider risk or volatility. For that we need percent risk.
- Percent risk: Risk a predetermined percentage of equity per trade. If we close a trade in which we lose the entire amount we risk, we lose a percentage of total equity. We look at the past to define the algorithm

for the actual sizing by incorporating volatility into the calculation. We can define the risk more carefully. The risk is based on the entry price minus the stop-loss price. When we get stopped out we will lose exactly what we risk (though slippage and gaps can cause you to lose more).

In this way we treat the volatility of each stock individually and can risk the same dollar amount on different stocks. We risk the same amount per stock by varying the size of the position; our position in low volatile stocks can be larger than the size of high volatile stocks.

I like to combine both percent risk and percent size. With percent risk we can potentially take much larger positions in a low-volatility stock than we could with percentage size. However, there is always the chance of a price shock, like the $30 stock that we bought opening at $15 the next day.

Here's an example of how a percent risk sizing calculation works. Let's assume the following:

- Stock price: $30
- Average True Range: $2
- Stop-loss: 2 Average True Range
- If we enter at 30 then the stop-loss price will be: $30 – (2 x $2) = $26
- Percent risk per trade: 2%

This means that each position risks 2 percent of our equity. The calculation of this is as follows:

- Equity: $100,000
- Risk per trade: 2%
- Dollar risk per position: 2% x $100,000 = $2,000

Remember, our risk is calculated by the difference between the entry price and stop-loss price. If the entry is at $30 and our stop-loss is $26, then we have a dollar risk per share of $4. Here's how we calculate our desired position:

- Total dollar risk/dollar risk per share = position size
- In our example, $2,000/$4 = 500 shares

We use this type of position sizing so that we know exactly what percentage of our equity we can lose on each position. However, we have not yet defined our total position size, just our risk per trade. In the previous example, we entered the stock at $30, and our stop-loss was set at $26, but there's a chance that an overnight news event could cause the stock to open at, say, $24. If that happens, our stop is irrelevant; we will suffer a large loss at the open price of $24. Therefore, we must limit our maximum size as well to a point that our risk is comfortable even if we lose more than we are planning with our stop-loss.

When we only use percent risk, we define our position sizing based on past volatility. Of course, it's good to base our sizing on volatility—however, we're using the past, and we don't know if the future will be the same. That's the drawback of this method.

Remember, too, in times of low volatility, the stop is set based on the volatility. The lower the volatility, the smaller the stop size, and the smaller the stop size, the larger the total position, which can result in a position that is too large compared to your entire portfolio.

To combat these two issues and keep risk acceptable, we limit the total position size to a set percentage of total equity. We have already decided that we would not take a position greater than 10 percent of total equity. In this example, we have calculated via percent risk that we could buy 500 shares:

- 500 shares x $30 = $15,000, or 15% of our equity

We limit this too-large position by layering on a percent-size calculation. This adapts the position to 10 percent of our equity. The formula is:

- Total equity x maximum percent of equity per position = equity per position
- Then, equity per position/share price = number of shares in the position

So, the final size is for our trade is:

- $100,000 x 10% = $10,00, then $10,000/$30 = 333 shares

In all the systems I describe in this book, I set a maximum of ten positions per system so we can have a maximum of 100 percent allocated per system Here's why: Imagine the system tells me to buy ten stocks one day, but only three of the orders are filled. Then imagine that the next day it sees another ten setups. If I have not set my parameters to limit my positions to a total of ten, and all of my new orders are filled, now I have thirteen positions in my system. This can continue, causing margin issues.

Position sizing is incredibly important. It is a way to define your objectives, and also to manage your risk. You must think about this before you begin trading. You must think about how much you are willing to risk. A trader can have a great strategy, go live, and the account begins losing more money than they expected or are prepared for. Now they are no longer trading in a rational way.

Too-aggressive position sizing can cause people to judge their systems based on how much money they lose, rather than whether they are conceptually sound and valid.

Position sizing can shape your objectives, but if you haven't been clear about your objectives, the wrong sizing can really hurt you. You can build great systems and still ruin your account because you are not emotionally prepared for the drawdowns your position sizing permits.

In one of our trend-following systems, Long High Momentum, we use the standard position sizing that we use for all systems, i.e., 2 percent percent risk and maximum 10 percent percent size of total equity. You can see how the results vary when we change these algorithms:

Table 9: Effect of Varying Percent Risk and Maximum Percent Size on Results

Percent risk of total equity	Maximum percent size of total equity	Ending Balance	CAGR%	Max Total Equity DD	MAR
0.50%	10%	756,115.79	8.59%	15.10%	0.57
0.75%	10%	1,698,642.16	12.23%	19.70%	0.62
1.00%	10%	3,166,436.78	15.11%	25.30%	0.6
1.25%	10%	5,053,661.46	17.32%	30.50%	0.57
1.50%	10%	7,542,769.29	19.25%	34.90%	0.55
1.75%	10%	10,868,072.73	21.04%	38.70%	0.54
2.00%	10%	14,660,643.97	22.52%	42.10%	0.53
2.25%	10%	18,440,243.45	23.67%	45.20%	0.52
2.50%	10%	21,718,577.33	24.50%	48.20%	0.51
2.75%	10%	24,585,004.33	25.13%	51.10%	0.49
3.00%	10%	25,823,065.57	25.38%	53.60%	0.47
0.50%	15%	757,457.29	8.60%	15.10%	0.57
0.75%	15%	1,716,187.58	12.27%	19.70%	0.62
1.00%	15%	3,544,090.87	15.64%	25.40%	0.62
1.25%	15%	6,528,640.11	18.55%	30.60%	0.61
1.50%	15%	10,944,375.72	21.07%	35.40%	0.6
1.75%	15%	16,402,708.10	23.08%	39.90%	0.58
2.00%	15%	23,600,768.76	24.92%	43.90%	0.57
2.25%	15%	32,420,452.68	26.55%	47.40%	0.56
2.50%	15%	43,766,772.63	28.10%	50.50%	0.56
2.75%	15%	57,703,878.22	29.55%	53.50%	0.55
3.00%	15%	72,555,715.52	30.77%	56.10%	0.55

With the exact same buy and sell decisions, the same trades we see differences as much as a lowest CAGR of 8.59 percent with a maximum drawdown of only 15.10 percent or the very aggressive alternative (that many times will trade on margin) with a 30.77 percent CAGR and a 56.10 percent maximum drawdown.

Chapter 6

The 12 Ingredients of Every Trading System

No matter the system, it should contain all of these ingredients:

1. Your objectives

2. Your beliefs

3. Trading universe

4. Filters

5. Setup

6. Ranking

7. Entry

8. Stop-loss

9. Reentry

10. Profit protection

11. Profit taking

12. Position sizing

Let's explore each of these.

1) Objectives

The first ingredient of every trading system is your objectives, which I discussed in chapter 4. I encourage you to think deeply about them, and to write yours out.

2) Beliefs

We can only trade a system if we believe it will make money, so we need a core belief for that system. What are the thought processes behind the buy-and-sell engine that actually make conceptual sense? An example of a belief could be that I believe I want to enter into a stock when it is clearly trending up, I will have a trailing stop-loss, and I will stick with that position until the trend bends. This is a belief about price action. A fundamentals trader such as Warren Buffett may buy the same stock, but his belief is rooted in his expectation that the stock will rise because of his interpretation of the fundamentals of that particular company—for example, he believes the management team is exceptionally skilled, or he sees growing profits as the company expands into new markets. We, on the other hand, trade on price action, which pays no attention to fundamentals such as these—sometimes I don't even know what company is represented by the symbol I am trading.

Another belief is that if I see a stock that has really been pummeled in the short term, say over the last four days, I may believe that there is a higher-than-average statistical likelihood that it will bounce back and return to its mean. I can play the exact opposite belief on the short side: if I see a stock has jumped up in the last few days and looks overbought, I can short it with the belief that it, too, will return to its mean. Again, these are beliefs based on price action, not fundamentals. I can turn these beliefs into specific buy and sell rules to create my buy-and-sell engine.

Beliefs ↔ Backtesting

Remember that your beliefs (and the other eleven ingredients) are like algorithms that you backtest. You'll have statistical evidence that your beliefs give you an edge, at least in the past. If you don't find an edge in your trading, you revisit your results and refine your beliefs, and your systems. Beliefs and backtesting results evolve together.

3) Trading Universe

What are you going to trade? You can trade the components of an index, for example, or a basket of stocks, or ETFs, and so on. Different instruments have different pros and cons.

When you're thinking about your trading universe, you must first consider your system. For example, some people might have a belief that they like to trade long in the S&P 500 because they believe the best companies are included there, and the worst companies are moved out of the index. The index embodies a continuous survivorship bias that should help them. On the other hand, if we trade a higher-frequency, mean reversion system where we need a lot of short-term trades to achieve a good CAGR, the S&P 500 most likely doesn't offer enough stocks to work with. In that case we'll need a larger universe of stocks.

Or, if we had a small account and wanted to be in the next Google, Netflix or Microsoft, before the big institutional traders get involved, we'd need a huge trading universe, probably all 7,000 listed stocks in the United States, rather than a particular index.

We answer the question of trading universe by answering the question, "what kind of stocks do I want to be in?"

4) Filters

Filters help refine and answer exactly that question. If we were to trade the entire S&P 500, or all listed stocks, setups would come in large multiples because the market is fairly correlated.

We need to have a way to filter out the stocks we are not interested in. The first logical filter is liquidity. What kind of volume does the stock have?

Traders at big institutions use filters that ensure they meet their own standards. For example, they may not be allowed to trade a stock with a daily volume of less than a million shares, because those stocks may not have enough liquidity for the size of the trades the institution needs to enter, or the institution's trade may move the market, erasing its edge.

People with small accounts—and by small I mean less than $5 million—can have a huge edge because they trade underneath the radar of the institutional traders. If you're trading a $50,000 account, you can definitely trade stocks that trade a few hundred thousand shares per day and find a huge edge.

Liquidity filters look at average share volume and average dollar volume. Another useful filter is price. Again, institutional traders have rules. Often they can't trade a stock priced below $10. These stocks tend to be more volatile, and many times we see more irrational behavior and more gamblers trading them, which can give us an edge in shorter-term trades.

You can also consider maximum price. If you have a smaller account, you probably don't want to be trading stocks that cost $600 or $700 per share, because it is harder to get your position sizing right.

Volatility is another important filter. We need volatility; if we only trade stocks that barely move, we can't make any money. Volatility is our friend because we're able to size our position to be within our comfort zone, yet we can make money. I trade stocks that are incredibly volatile, but the relative size of the position is not that big, so it doesn't concern me. A stock that is priced at $1 behaves very differently than a stock priced at $30. I have to size my position to allow for that, so I can capture the volatility.

5) Setup

This is where we measure the price action of the stock to define what stocks we want to be in. We use quantified rules through technical indicators that measure price action.

You select technical indicators and use those to convert your belief into a simple algorithm. For example, if you believe you want to buy stocks in an uptrend, then we can measure the market by a simple moving average. If the close is above that moving average, the market is in an uptrend. That is a simple belief turned into a simple uptrend. Another one: if we want to buy stocks that have been oversold in the short term, we can set a simple rule that selects stocks that have dropped 12.5 percent in the last three days (that's not even an indicator, it just uses raw price action.)

There are many technical indicators. Understand that there are no magical indicators. They do not exist. A lot of people in the trading education industry want you to believe that you need their magic indicator. That's is not the case, because the only thing any indicator measures is the past price action of a stock. That's all it does. It does not predict the future. The only thing you can be sure about regarding the future is that it will be different. At best, it gives an indication of the future.

Setups quantify what kinds of price history characteristics we want to see in the stocks we will trade. Now we have a list of stocks that are good candidates.

6) Ranking

You may very well have more setups than you want to take positions in. That's where the incredibly important step of ranking comes in.

Ranking is how we prioritize which stock to trade when we have more setups than our maximum number of positions allows us to trade.

Let's say we're trading a trend-following system in the S&P 500 and it's a huge bull market. Because the market many times can be correlated, many stocks will be set up as candidates. Many times I've seen situations where I measure a trend in the S&P 500 and I find 100 or 150 candidate stocks to buy. If your position sizing tells you that you can only buy 10 stocks, you need to figure out which of those 150 to trade.

You might rank stocks by:

- Volatility
- Strongest trend
- Most overbought
- Most oversold

Because you're only trading ten stocks, the ranking is a very important part of your system. If you choose the most volatile stocks, or the most overbought stocks, or the most oversold stocks, you will come up with very different rankings. This brings you back to your beliefs. If you are trading a trend-following system, for example, your beliefs about which stocks will perform well in that trend will inform the way you filter.

7) Entry

Do you want a guaranteed entry—to be in the stock no matter the price? Then set an entry rule to buy at market on open. You can have a little slippage with this approach (the price you get might not be the price you expected), but if the trade is going to be of long duration and you want to make sure you're in it, that's not an issue.

For short-term systems, I like to enter with a limit order, which specifies the price I'll pay. I might set a limit of $20, and the stock opens at $20.15. The order won't be filled. That's okay, because with short-term trades that have smaller profit margins, I need good order fills or I erode my edge. I can't afford a lot of slippage. (When you backtest, be sure to incorporate a conservative slippage estimate on market orders, or your results will look better than they would have in live trading.)

If I want to make sure a stock is moving in the right direction before I buy, I can look at the $20 price of the stock and put a stop in at $20.15, combined with a market order. If the stock rises enough that the price crosses $20.15, my order is executed at the market price.

8) Stop-Loss

Stop-loss is the price at which we get out if the trade is going against us and we want to protect our capital. It is key to always know your exit point before you enter a trade so that you always know what your maximum loss is. The trade is not working out, so we get out and look for another opportunity. As you've seen, we need stop-losses to define our risk. If you have a 10 percent stop-loss in a stock that ends up dropping 30 percent, you're going to feel pretty good that you got out when you did.

What about not using stops?

Some traders will argue that backtested results of systems are better if they use no stop-loss. While that may be true on paper, it exposes you to ruin. You have no way to protect your capital. Psychologically, do you want that, even if there is the chance for greater returns? Even if it looks better on backtested results, we need to understand that the future will be different and what has *not* happened in the past might happen in the future.

When setting a stop-loss, it's essential to set it outside the trading noise. Every day a stock experiences a certain amount of trading noise as it moves up and down within a limited range. If you put your stop too close to your entry price, you can be stopped out by a relatively minor change in price that didn't actually represent significant movement. Too many times, traders set their stops too close, get stopped out on a minor downturn, then watch as the stock rises significantly without them.

9) Reentry

What is your plan if you get stopped out of a stock at a loss, or you get out at your pre-established profit target, and the next day the system tells you to get back into the stock? This can be a bit psychologically challenging, but through backtesting I have seen in my systems that I should do the trade. What happened yesterday has no bearing on what will happen today, so if my system tells me that this is a good trade, I take it.

All the systems in this book are set to reenter.

10) Profit Protection

Profit protection ensures we will capture at least some of our profit, while still holding the door open to a stock going higher. On a trend following long system, a trailing stop follows the rising price of your stock and is a form of profit protection. Once a long-term trend bends, you give back some of the profit (because the stop is outside the noise), and eventually get stopped out. This works whether you are trend following long or short.

As I've noted, you have to be willing to leave enough space in your stop. On a trend following system it's common to have a trailing stop of 15–25 percent of the highest price. If you don't, you may miss out on a big winner that goes on an extended run but has 10 percent or 15 percent pullbacks during that run. (Note that the trailing stop-loss may be a separate stop from what you put in place when you first entered the trade.)

Mean reversion systems do not have a profit protection mechanism because you get out of the trade in only a few days, either by hitting a profit target, hitting a time-based exit, or being stopped out.

11) Profit Taking

This is something to use in short-term mean reversion systems; you set a profit target where you'll get out. Let's say you get in at $20 and set a 5 percent profit target. When it goes to $21, you're out. I pair this with a time stop—that is, I get out regardless of what that stock has done in a certain number of days, often three or four. The stock will either revert quickly to the mean, and I'll make a profit, or I'll get stopped out at a loss, or I'll get timed out and go look for some other opportunity. On shorter term trades you want to get in, get a profit or not, and get out. What counts here is a large trade frequency and time stops help with that.

As long as you have a consistent and significant edge that taking profit is more profitable than random, and your average winning trade is better than your average losing trade, then you have a very good system.

12) Position Sizing

If you didn't read chapter 5, now is the time, because position sizing is critical to achieving your risk and return objectives. It is the last of the twelve key ingredients in every trading system.

In the seven trading systems I describe in the following chapters, three of these ingredients stay the same: trading universe, reentry, and position sizing. I do this so that it is easier to compare the performance of the various systems.

Chapter 7

Increasing Risk-Adjusted Return by Combining Multiple Noncorrelated Systems

Systems 1, 2 and 3

We begin an evaluation of the strength of multiple noncorrelated systems with our benchmark: the performance of the S&P 500. As a reminder, here it is again.

Table 2: S&P 500 Performance, 1995-2019

January 2, 1995 – July 24, 2019	SPY
CAGR	8.02%
Maximum Drawdown	56.47%
Longest Drawdown	86.1 Months
Annualized Volatility	18.67%
Sharpe	0.43
MAR	0.14
Total Return	562.51%

As you can see, a buy-and-hold strategy in the SPY does in fact make money. From January 1995 to July 2019, it had a CAGR of 8 percent. However, the price you had to pay to attain that growth rate was a 56 percent maximum drawdown. In other words, during that time period you would lose, on paper, more than half of your money. Moreover, you were drawn down for eighty-six months—that's *more than seven years.*

Even our best performing systems spend a great deal of time in drawdown—that is, below their peak highs. No trader ever goes directly from one high to another indefinitely. However, the S&P 500 was in drawdown 93 percent of the time. So that's our benchmark.

Let's consider that for a moment. Who would like to be in a drawdown for seven years? People forget this. I have made this point before, but I will make it again, because if you can truly grasp this, you have a real edge as a trader. They have incredible recency bias. They forget that the drawdown in 2008 alone took six years to recover. Most people only can remember the last few years, and it's incredibly important that you remember what happens when the market really turns south, such as during the post-dot-com period. If you were invested just in the NASDAQ at that point, you didn't lose half your money—you lost three-quarters of your money! The NASDAQ was down 74 percent. Even if you were in the S&P 500, the truth is, if you bought and held in at the top of the year 2000, you didn't make any money for thirteen years. You briefly got back to where you started in 2008, and then it dropped again.

Thirteen years of drawdown before you saw growth again. Who can handle that? If you used an investment advisor you did worse, because you paid him fees. And just for fun, during that time you lost half your money—twice! That's a lot of pain for an 8 percent average annual return.

Remember this history. People tend to want to remember only the good times. The runup since 2009 has been great. Remember this history, and you will have the right mindset to build systems for whatever the future may bring.

Can we do better?

In this chapter I will introduce you to the first three of seven noncorrelated systems I describe in this book (many more are possible), show you how they work individually, and begin to show you how they work together.

For each of the systems I'll run through the ingredients for each system and show backtested results.

As with the previous systems I've discussed, I'm keeping position sizing constant to simplify comparison of performance between systems. More aggressive position sizing can increase returns, but it also increases risks. And, as before, we limit our maximum positions in a system at any one time to ten and the maximum equity allocation per position to 10 percent, so we don't have margin issues.

System 1: Long Trend High Momentum

- **Objectives:**
  - To be in trending stocks that have big momentum. This gets you into the high-fliers, the popular stocks, when the market is an uptrend. We only want to trade when the market sentiment is in our favor and we are in very liquid stocks. I like a lot of volume for long-term positions, because the volume may diminish over time and you want to have a cushion so you can always get out with good liquidity.
  - In this system I want the trend of the stock to be up in a very simple way. Nothing fancy. Also, I like to rank this system with the more volatile stocks first.
  - And I want a guaranteed entry—I'm not too worried about slippage because this is a long position, and I've calculated some slippage into my backtests anyway. I want to stay in the stock for a long ride up, so I'll have a wide trailing stop.
- **Beliefs:** Historical testing has shown that buying big momentum stocks has a consistent edge when bought in an uptrend and then putting in a trailing stop to capture profits.
- **Trading Universe:** All stocks listed on the NYSE, NASDAQ, and AMEX.
- **Filter:**
  - Average daily dollar volume greater than $50 million over the last twenty days.
  - Minimum price $5.00. I don't like trading stocks that have a price below $5.00 because I believe they can be too volatile, but I do believe I have an edge trading stocks below $10, because the

institutionals usually are not involved.

- **Setup:**
  - Close of the SPY is above the 100-day simple moving average (SMA). This indicates a trend in the overall index.
  - The close of the 25-day simple moving average is above the close of the 50-day simple moving average.
- **Ranking:** In case we have more setups than our position sizing allows, we rank by the highest rate of change over the last 200 trading days. This means the highest percentage price increase over the last 200 trading days. This means we'll be into stocks that are definitely on the monitors of CNBC. We're joining the crowd with the expectation that things will keep going up.
- **Entry:** Next day market order on open. I'm not worried about slippage for a long trade, and I definitely want to be in.
- **Stop-Loss:** The day after entering the trade, place a stop-loss below the execution price of five times the average true range (ATR) of the last twenty days. That will definitely keep me outside the daily noise and give the trade room to develop.
- **Reentry:** If stopped out, reenter the next day if all entry conditions apply again.
- **Profit Protection:** A trailing stop of 25 percent. This is in addition to the initial stop-loss. Eventually, as the stock rises, the trailing stop will move up above the stop-loss price.
- **Profit taking:** No profit target; the goal is to ride this as high as it will go.
- **Position sizing:** 2 percent risk and 10 percent maximum percentage size, with a maximum of ten positions.

Table 10: Results for Long Trend High Momentum

January 2, 1995 – July 24, 2019	Trading System
CAGR%	22.52%
Maximum Drawdown	42.14%
Annualized Volatility	22.70%
Sharpe	0.99
MAR	0.53
Win%	45.66%
Win/Loss	3.24
Avg Days in Trade	213.02
Total Return	14,560.64%

With a compound annual growth rate of 22.52 percent, you can see this system alone is almost three times better than the 8 percent SPY CAGR. However, the maximum drawdown is 42 percent, which is better than the S&P 500, but still too high. We see a win rate of 45 percent, in the normal range for long-term trend following systems, which generally win less than 50 percent of the time. The Win/Loss Ratio shows you how the system makes money; the average winning trade made 3.24 times as much money as the average losing trade lost. The strength of the system lies in cutting out the losers and letting the winners run, and you can see that we were in trades for an average of 213 days. That's a high number, indicating this is a system with a low turnover. Generally the higher this number, for an LTTF system, the better, as it indicates we are staying with winners longer.

The historic volatility—22.7 percent versus the S&P's 18 percent—indicates that this would be a more volatile ride. I include the Sharpe and MAR numbers because many traders like to use them and they are a quick shorthand for comparing systems.

Chart 15: Equity Curve for Long Trend High Momentum

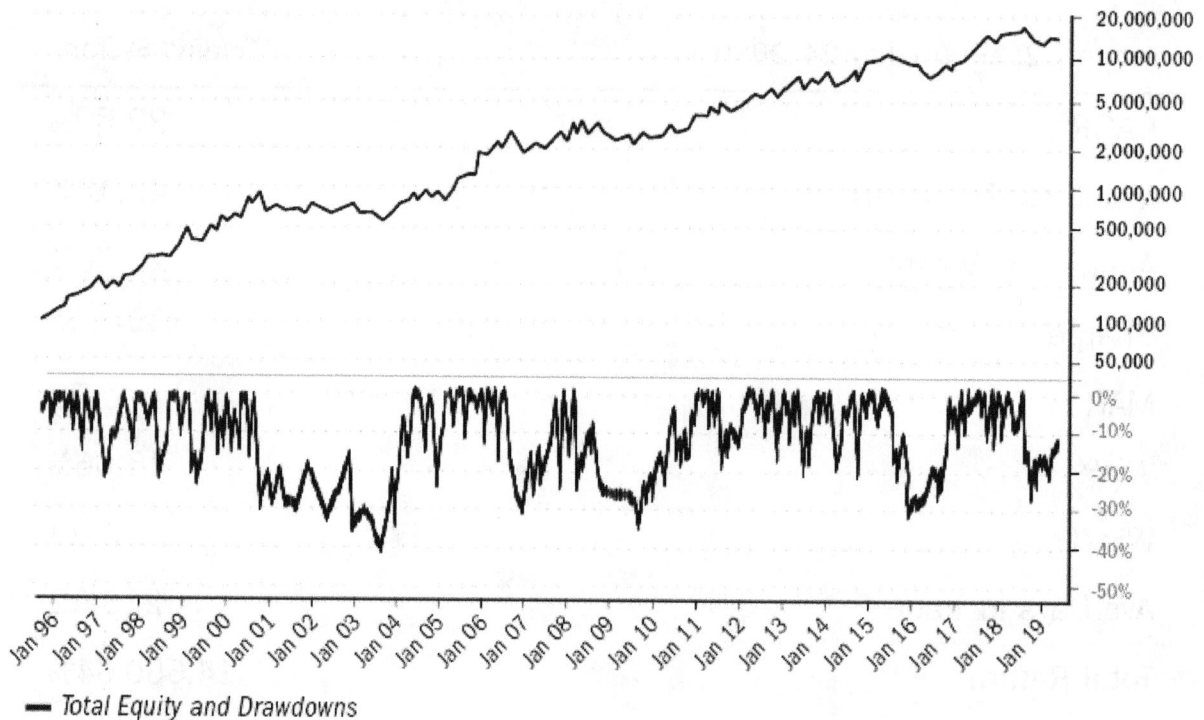

— *Total Equity and Drawdowns*

In our hypothetical system we start with $100,000 in January 1995 and this is how the equity develops over time. This kind of performance is typical for trend following. We get drawdowns in bear and sideways markets. It's impossible to make money and we start to lose some. In addition, at times when the S&P index is below the 100-day simple moving average we don't get any set ups and thus don't get any new trades. Then we are on the sidelines and know it will take a long time to recover from that drawdown. When there are no trends there are no setups, and this is one of the biggest drawbacks of trend following systems but also exactly where the edge is. We only trade long when the odds are more in our favor for these systems.

This system can look great on paper, with a nice compounded annual growth rate, but in live trading it can be hard to trade. Someone might look at the graph and tell themselves, "I could handle that 42 percent drawdown to get a 22.5 percent compounded annual growth rate." Let's say the person started to trade in March 2000, exactly when that drawdown happened. They would need to withstand a drawdown of five years. Most people can't handle that pain. So, by itself it is a system that is far superior to the S&P 500 or Warren Buffett's fund, but it is only the beginning of what we are going to end up with when we start to combine it with other noncorrelating systems.

System 2: Short RSI Thrust

- **Objective:** Short stocks in order to hedge when the markets move down. When long positions start to lose money, this system should offset those losses. This is the perfect add-on to an LTTF system, to capture those downward moves.
- **Beliefs:** There is always a time when there's so much greed in certain stocks that when you short them, the statistical likelihood that you can buy them back a few days later at a lower price is greater than random, so there's a very consistent edge.
- **Trading Universe:** All listed stocks on the NYSE, NASDAQ, and AMEX. We want as many opportunities as possible to find stocks that fit our criteria. Because this system is built from very short-term trades with small profits, we need to complete many trades in a year. The more trades, the higher the CAGR.
- **Filter:**
    - Minimum price of $5.00. Penny stocks don't appeal to me, because they can move up and down violently, especially overnight.
    - Average dollar volume over the last twenty days greater than $25 million. We need enough volume to generate the liquidity necessary for you to be able to short the stock. Without sufficient volume, your broker might deny a request for a short.
    - Average true range percentage over the last ten days is 3 percent or more of the closing price of the stock. This filter identifies stocks that have sufficient volatility for the system to work. Measuring ATR as a percentage of the closing price treats every stock the same in terms of assessing their volatility.
- **Setup:**
    - Three-day RSI is above ninety. This shows a lot of demand and momentum for the stock—another way of saying "a lot of greed."
    - The last two days the close was higher than the previous day. Each day the stock is closing higher, which gives me an opportunity to go against the herd mentality of people piling into

the stock.

- **Ranking:** Highest seven-day ADX. The ADX helps us to select stocks that are moving a lot, and many times a very high ADX is a good indication of a trend reversal.
- **Entry:** Next day, sell short 4 percent above the previous closing price. This is a limit price, to ensure we don't have negative slippage, which could erode our edge. Also, selling short 4 percent higher than the previous close gives us an additional edge, capturing more intraday greed.
- **Stop-Loss:** The day after we place the order, place a buy stop of three times ATR of the last ten days above the execution price. This is a large stop, but it is the key for mean reversion. If the stock continues to rise, we will be stopped out, buying back the stock we shorted at three times the ATR. I have seen a lot of traders, even professional traders, put too small a stop-loss because they are greedy and don't want to lose that much. This can destroy the edge. We are in stocks that are very much in the market favor, and we cannot expect that the moment we short them they are going to begin to drop back toward their mean. They may continue to rise. We need a lot of space to allow the stock to hit that point of exhaustion and for a selloff to begin. Backtesting shows that this system performs best without any stop-loss in place, but I don't like to trade a system where I cannot manage risk. Theoretically this system can move up infinitely against us.
- **Reentry:** If we get stopped out, reenter the next day if all entry conditions apply again.
- **Profit Protection:** None. No trailing stop because it is a very short-term trade.
- **Profit Taking:**
  - If at the closing price the profit in the position is 4 percent or higher, get out the next day's market on close.
  - We also have a time-based exit: If after two days the trade has not reached its profit target, we place a market order on close for the next day. The goal is to make a fast profit or get out of the position. If we stay in the position it may go against us. Instead, let's get out and look for another candidate.
- **Position Sizing:** 2 percent risk and 10 percent size, a maximum of ten positions.

Table 11: Results for Short RSI Thrust

January 2, 1995 – July 24, 2019	Trading System
CAGR%	18.14%
Maximum Drawdown	24.66%
Annualized Volatility	11.50%
Sharpe	1.58
MAR	0.74
Win%	5.84%
Win/Loss	0.98
Daily Return Correlation to Benchmark	-0.28
Total Return	5,897.58%

This is a very good system by itself. It has an 18 percent CAGR and a 24.66 percent maximum drawdown. The win rate is almost 58 percent, and the Win/Loss ratio is close to 1.00, which is typical for these types of systems; mean reversion systems make their money because they have more wins than losses. The most important statistic here is the Daily Return Correlation to Benchmark, which is negative. This is exactly what we want; it means it makes money when the market is going down. That's the performance we're looking for, because we will combine this with a system that makes money as the market is going up (Long Trend High Momentum).

Chart 16: Equity Curve for Short RSI Thrust

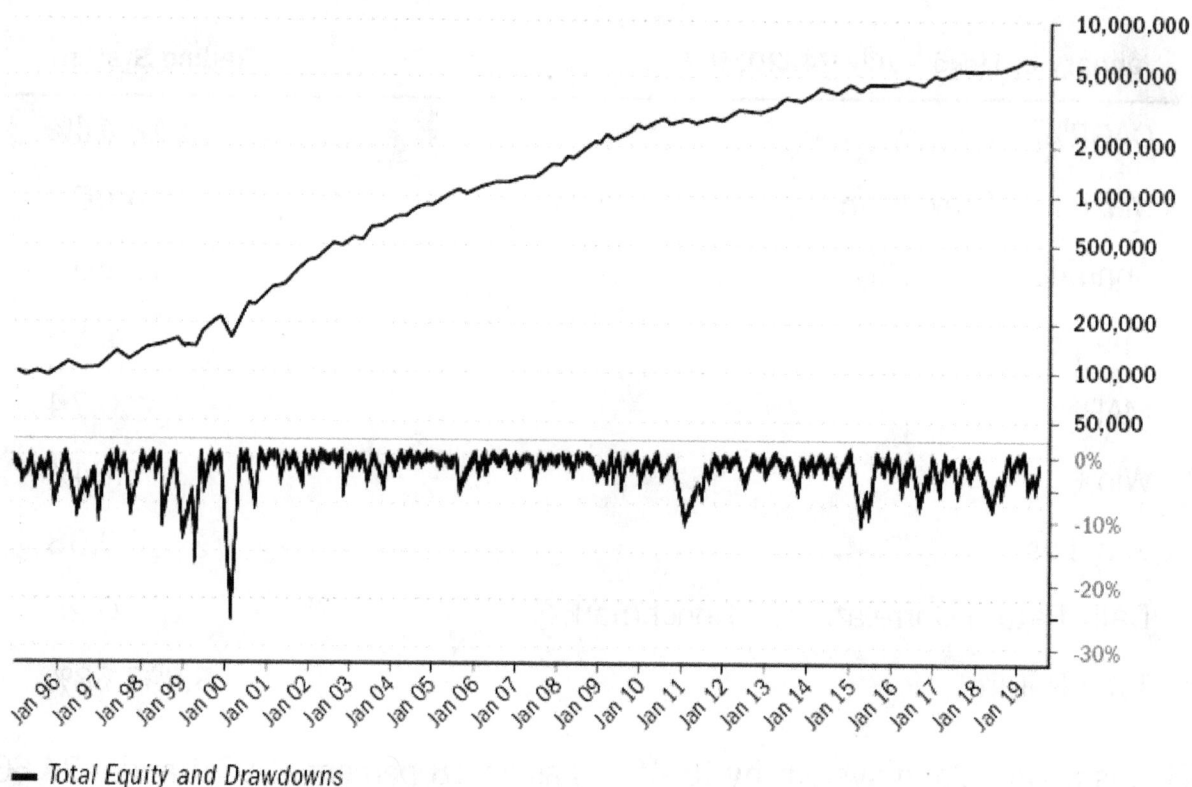

— Total Equity and Drawdowns

Now we have developed one long and one short system and the results were as follows:

Table 12: Individual Systems Performance

Trading System	CAGR%	Max DD	MAR	Sharpe
Long Trend – High momentum	22.52	42.14%	0.53	0.99
Short RSI Thrust	18.14	24.66%	0.74	1.58

In the graphic above I have summarized the performance of System 1: Long Trend High Momentum, and System 2: Short RSI Thrust. Now let's imagine we trade these systems simultaneously, so we are 100 percent long and 100 percent short. This would mean that we trade on leverage, but that's fine because your long systems covers your short systems. When we are 100 percent long and the market has moved up, the long positions will generally make money, the short positions will lose a little. If we trade 100 percent long and 100 percent short, the net exposure will be near zero, because they tend to balance each other out. Many times we are not 100 percent exposed on either side. At a maximum investment level we would be 100 percent long and short together, but we might be something more like 70 percent long 30 percent short. We make better use of equity when we use more equity for each system, and since both systems are pointed a different direction, they are basically inversely correlated.

Both of these systems have a clear edge. But now let's see how they would combine when we trade the simultaneously, which means we trade at the same time 100 percent long and 100 percent short:

Table 13: Combined Systems Performance

Trading System	CAGR%	Max DD	MAR	Sharpe
Combined long and short, both 100%	43.54	31.5%	1.38	2.11

Here you can begin to see the power of multiple noncorrelated systems trading. At almost 43 percent, the CAGR is substantially improved compared to either of the individual systems. The maximum drawdown is now 31 percent, the MAR is a healthy 1.38, and the longest drawdown is 16.5 months.

Table 14: Long Trend High Momentum and Short RSI Thrust Combined Results

January 2, 1995 – July 24, 2019	Trading System	SPY
CAGR%	43.54%	8.02%
Maximum Drawdown	31.54%	56.47%
Longest Drawdown	16.5 Months	86 Months
Annualized Volatility	20.67%	18.67%
Sharpe	2.11	0.43
MAR	1.38	0.14
Total Return	714,804.60%	562.51%

Chart 17: Equity Curve of 100% Long Trend High Momentum and 100% Short RSI Thrust Combined Results

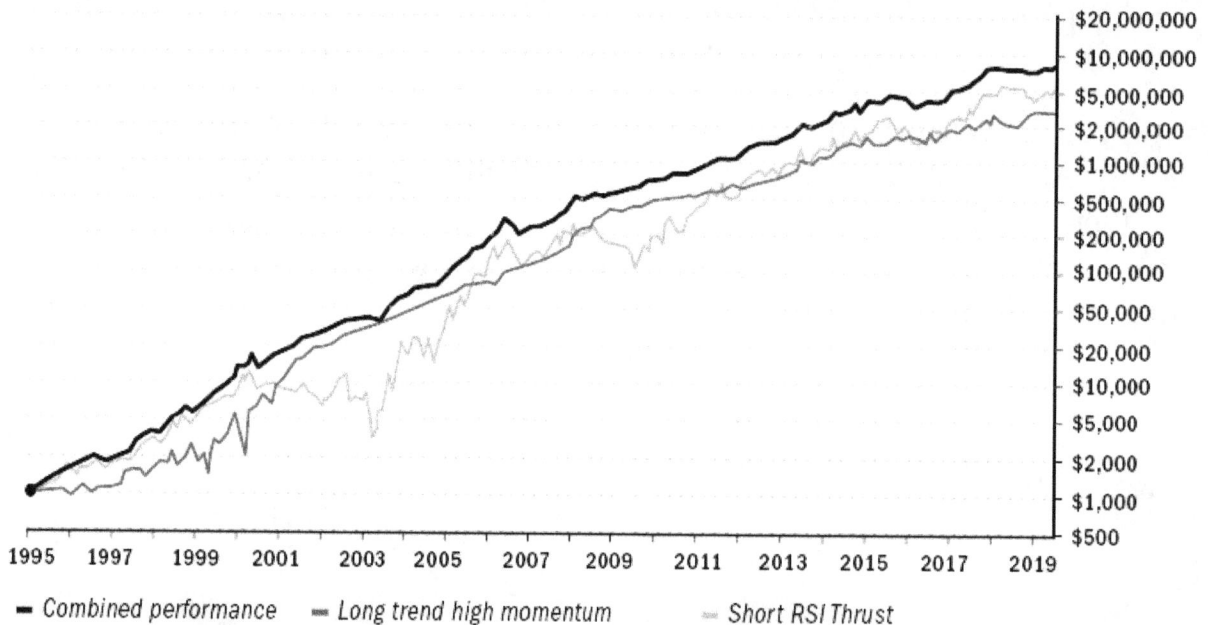

— Combined performance   — Long trend high momentum   — Short RSI Thrust

Comparing our combined systems to the S&P 500 benchmark, we see substantially better performance on every measure except volatility which is slightly higher. Combined noncorrelated systems are absolutely the biggest edge we can have in trading.

In simplest terms, one system makes money when the other one doesn't, and those results combined produce superior performance compared to the benchmark. You can see in these charts that the equity curve begins to smooth out, and a smoother ride is a better ride.

Table 15: Combined Monthly Results, Long Trend High Momentum and Short RSI Thrust

%	JAN	FEB	MAR	APR	MAY	JUN	JUL	AUG	SEP	OCT	NOV	DEC	ANNUAL	SPY	COMPARISON
1995	01.17	4.01	9.88	0.90	5.73	6.84	6.21	15.08	16.44	-4.90	-0.87	-0.51	**74.19**	35.16	**39.03**
1996	4.40	7.87	3.62	2.91	-0.38	-4.66	-8.51	2.33	7.06	3.51	4.87	-3.02	**20.35**	20.31	**0.04**
1997	5.93	-0.97	3.03	15.34	8.50	8.11	7.16	0.69	8.03	-12.86	3.04	6.18	**62.52**	31.39	**31.14**
1998	6.82	11.08	9.19	9.59	-0.13	14.04	4.11	-12.34	7.93	-1.04	9.50	6.31	**83.50**	27.04	**56.46**
1999	8.61	0.78	11.52	11.09	6.26	4.74	-0.35	5.96	2.73	11.49	15.27	16.72	**145.55**	19.11	**126.44**
2000	-16.07	12.45	-2.83	-5.51	5.81	6.90	4.48	5.30	3.93	-0.58	2.73	4.77	**19.93**	-10.68	**30.61**
2001	1.79	6.22	3.95	6.39	9.00	3.65	-1.35	3.29	-0.14	4.13	0.66	4.03	**49.86**	-12.87	**62.73**
2002	6.70	3.48	-0.35	9.16	3.91	0.35	-3.70	3.56	1.30	-1.72	5.37	-3.59	**26.32**	-22.81	**49.13**
2003	-7.63	4.97	3.06	2.92	8.31	13.58	5.19	7.99	9.97	9.66	0.50	1.11	**76.11**	26.12	**49.98**
2004	12.60	-0.16	-1.61	-1.06	3.23	7.77	-8.40	2.81	10.80	6.00	15.79	9.94	**71.40**	8.94	**62.46**
2005	0.37	10.54	7.33	-6.89	11.53	8.70	11.08	2.25	4.55	4.00	13.86	2.61	**93.96**	3.01	**90.95**
2006	8.80	-7.49	16.72	-0.54	11.46	-7.91	-5.67	-9.36	0.52	7.93	7.91	1.46	**21.78**	13.74	**8.04**
2007	6.03	-1.53	-2.08	5.48	9.31	6.92	0.79	0.90	11.84	14.73	-3.72	13.81	**80.25**	3.24	**77.00**
2008	-10.02	5.60	1.27	1.82	2.34	6.17	1.86	-4.83	-1.94	1.42	2.30	4.75	**9.98**	-38.28	**48.26**
2009	-0.33	0.10	0.00	3.49	-0.16	-1.13	2.82	6.12	6.92	-0.23	6.11	0.23	**26.13**	23.49	**2.64**
2010	-2.36	5.66	4.22	7.10	-2.36	0.28	0.69	-3.37	12.03	5.66	3.29	-1.60	**32.01**	12.84	**19.17**
2011	0.19	3.08	10.38	-1.66	4.83	3.22	4.70	-7.10	-1.44	6.21	1.26	0.04	**25.12**	-0.20	**25.32**
2012	7.88	4.91	8.87	6.07	4.15	-2.59	0.89	3.03	1.48	-2.49	1.06	3.36	**42.45**	13.47	**28.97**
2013	11.33	0.03	8.07	1.79	11.22	-6.54	3.77	-0.36	12.85	-2.78	5.69	-0.58	**51.78**	26.69	**22.09**
2014	0.15	13.47	-1.44	3.00	1.70	5.76	2.43	10.96	-7.38	-0.37	9.62	3.99	**48.69**	11.29	**37.40**
2015	2.14	-1.40	2.24	-6.66	9.50	5.03	3.44	-5.66	-6.24	1.81	6.12	-6.83	**1.81**	-0.81	**2.62**
2016	-9.86	-3.45	0.77	-3.33	4.54	12.48	1.96	-1.90	-0.46	-1.43	10.95	11.72	**21.27**	9.64	**11.63**
2017	0.27	0.77	3.00	-0.85	9.94	-2.19	8.97	5.43	8.46	9.32	0.29	-2.28	**48.12**	19.38	**28.63**
2018	12.27	-2.52	-2.62	-3.37	6.12	-2.77	1.15	4.36	4.93	-9.99	-3.45	-5.01	**-2.82**	-6.35	**3.53**
2019	5.64	4.85	7.98	-3.85	-6.65	6.46	6.68						**21.91**	20.61	**1.30**

This chart shows month-to-month performance. When you look at the annualized returns, they can look very attractive: almost all years show high double-digit returns, even 145 percent one year, and only one down year: 2018 by -2.82 percent. But you can also see a lot of down months, months where the combined system lost double digits. For instance, from June through August 2006 the system lost 30 percent of its value. Most people going through that would say, "I can't handle this, I'm done." While this performance chart shows good returns year-to-year, it's also a pretty wild ride. What we have here is good, but we can do better by reducing the volatility and increasing the risk adjusted return.

Lowering the overall volatility of a system, increasing the risk adjusted return (measured by MAR or Sharpe, for example) and increasing robustness is done by adding more non-correlating systems.

System 3: Long Mean Reversion Selloff

- **Objectives:** This is a long mean reversion system that is built to capture the majority of the pullbacks in an uptrend. We like to buy stocks in an uptrend, because that gives an edge. But if we wait for a pullback, when they become oversold, then the long edge becomes even greater. Note that while this is a long system, it is conceptually different from Long Trend High Momentum system. Although both systems are trading long, one is holding stocks for an average of over 200 days, while this one is in trades for only a few days, until the stock reverts to its mean. It's also different from the Short RSI Thrust system, because it's counting on oversold stocks going up, not stocks going down. When our systems are conceptually different, they take advantage of different market conditions and will not be closely correlated. This, by the way, is a mean reversion system that you can trade in IRA accounts, since it is a long system.
- **Beliefs:** Historical testing shows us that if we buy a stock that is dominated by fear and wait until it moves up, we definitely have an edge. It goes against human nature to buy a stock that suddenly goes into an apparent freefall, but backtesting shows there's a significant edge in doing so. My live trading has shown this concept to be very successful for the last thirteen years.
- **Trading Universe:** All listed stocks on the NYSE, NASDAQ, and AMEX. As with our other two systems, we want a large trading universe in order to have as many opportunities as possible. We'll need many trades, since each trade is designed to make a small, quick profit.
- **Filter:**
  - Minimum price of $1.00
  - Average volume over the last fifty days of 1 million shares.
  - Average true range over the last ten days is 5 percent or higher. This gets us into volatile stocks, which we need for this system to work.
- **Setup:**

- Close is above the 150-day Simple Moving Average
- The stock has dropped 12.5 percent or more in the last three days. This setup measures a significant downward move in an uptrending stock. You'll often see this kind of behavior when some kind of news event happens, such as a negative earnings report. Then, within a few days, traders realize this is actually a good stock to be in and they buy it again, sending it back up.

- **Ranking:** Stocks with the biggest drop over the last three days.
- **Entry:** Limit order of 7 percent below the previous closing price. This is important, because we are looking for stocks that are getting punished on intra-day trading. We are buying a falling knife. Inexperienced traders want to get out, but experienced traders want to get into a situation like this.
- **Stop-Loss:** 2.5 times the ATR of the last ten days below the execution price. This gives us a lot of space. We can't expect that we buy a stock 7 percent lower and straightaway the stock moves up and we make money. We want to have room for the stock to find bottom and begin to rebound, but we also want to limit our risk.
- **Reentry:** Yes
- **Profit Protection:** None
- **Profit Taking:** If profit is 4 percent or more based on the closing price, exit next day market on close. If after three days the stock has neither reached its profit target nor been stopped out, we place a market order to sell on close the following day.
- **Position Sizing:** 2 percent risk and 10 percent maximum percent size.

Table 16: Results for Long Mean Reversion Selloff

January 2, 1995 – July 24, 2019	Trading System
CAGR%	13.88%
Maximum Drawdown	13.83%
Longest Drawdown	43 months
Annualized Volatility	10.36%
Sharpe	1.34
MAR	1.00
Win%	63.04%
Win/Loss	0.88
Total Return	2,334.14%

The win rate was close to 63 percent, with a short trade duration and reduced drawdown. CAGR is close to double the benchmark, with almost half the volatility.

You can see that even in bear markets there were really not a lot of issues. Even in a bear market, there are violent up moves caused, for example, by short squeezes in individual stocks, and that's what the system is looking for.

Chart 18: Equity Curve for Long Mean Reversion Selloff

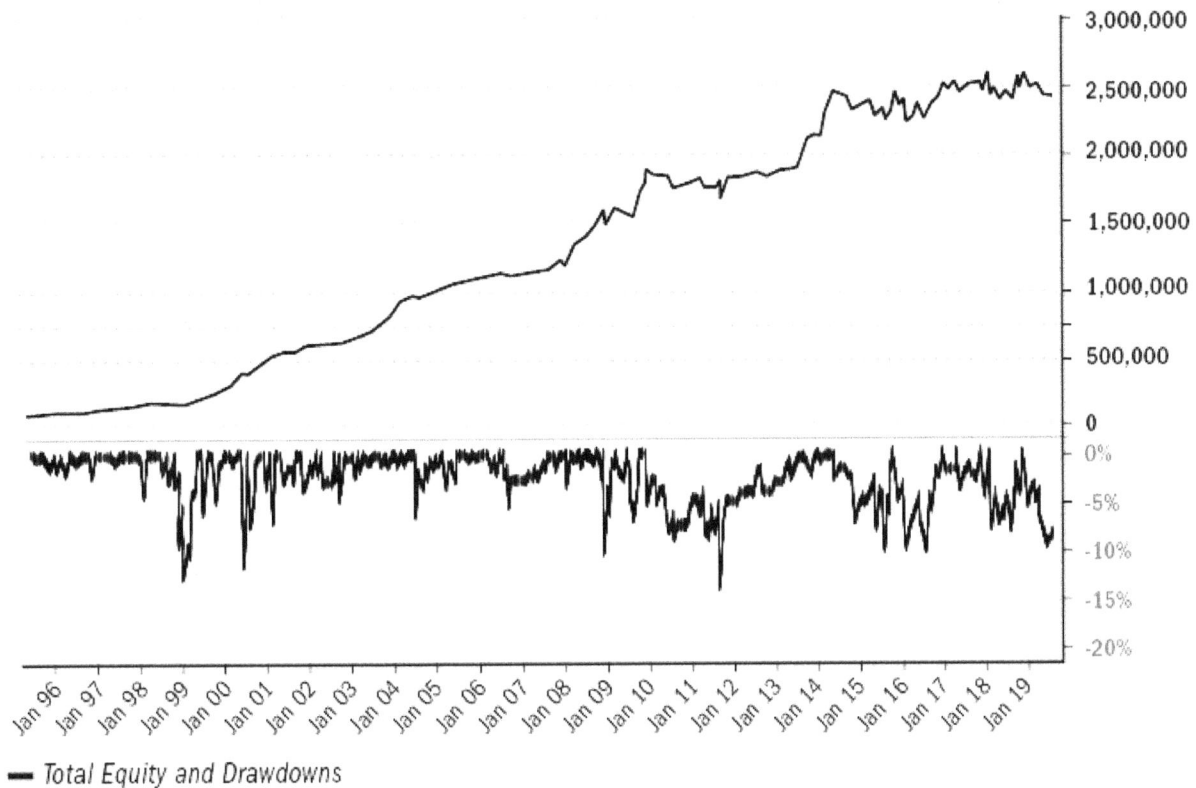

— Total Equity and Drawdowns

Now we combine all three systems, trading 50 percent mean reversion long, 50 percent long-term trend following, and 100 percent mean reversion short. We see increased performance in all the numbers. Risk adjusted return increases, the percentage of days in drawdown drops, and the size of drawdown drops. This is what we are seeking by combining multiple noncorrelated systems.

Table 17: Combined Results for 50% Long Trend High Momentum, 50% Mean Reversion Selloff, 100% Short RSI Thrust

January 2, 1995 – July 24, 2019	Trading System	SPY
CAGR%	39.59%	8.02%
Maximum Drawdown	19.33%	56.47%
Longest Drawdown	15.9 Months	86 Months
Annualized Volatility	15.11%	18.67%
Sharpe	2.62	0.43
MAR	2.05	0.14
Total Return	360,664.19%	562.51%

Chart 19: Equity Curve for 50% Long Trend High Momentum, 50% Mean Reversion Selloff, 100% Short RSI Thrust

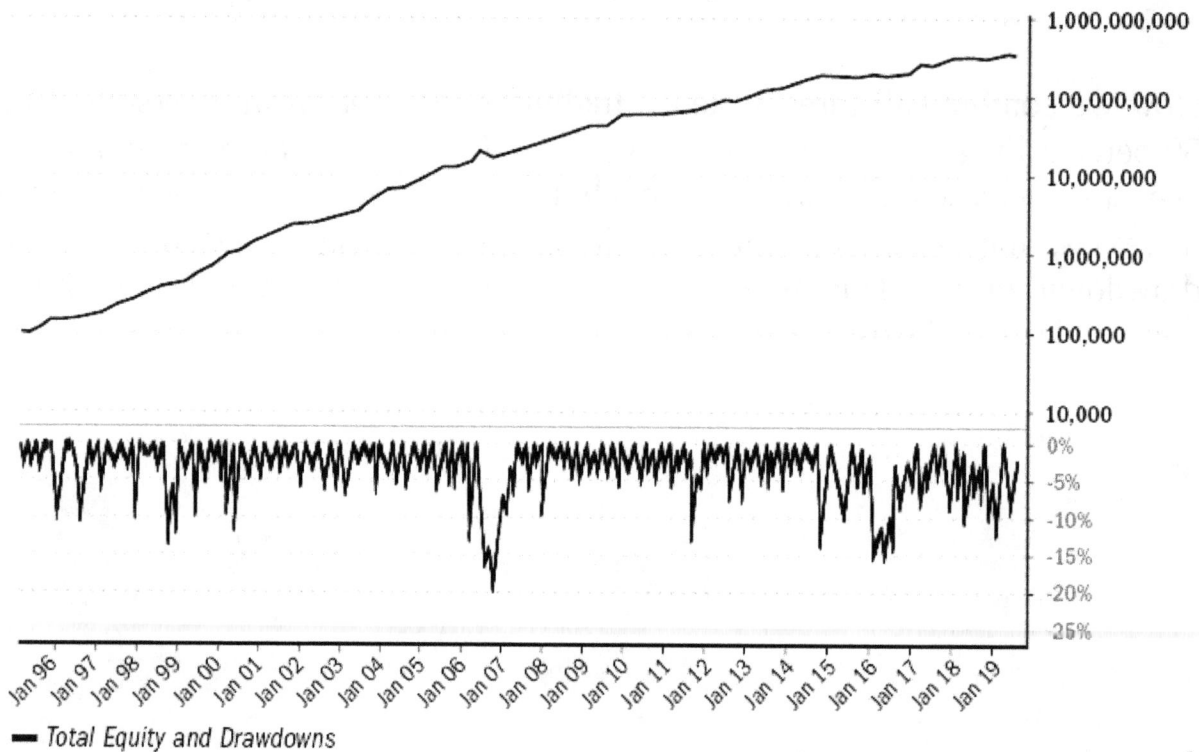

— *Total Equity and Drawdowns*

Table 18: Combined Monthly Results, Long Trend High Momentum, Mean Reversion Selloff and Short RSI Thrust

%	JAN	FEB	MAR	APR	MAY	JUN	JUL	AUG	SEP	OCT	NOV	DEC	ANNUAL	SPY	COMPARISON
1995	-0.26	1.27	7.00	1.01	3.83	4.15	3.94	9.12	11.21	-3.56	-1.80	-0.18	40.74	35.16	5.57
1996	3.96	5.76	4.15	1.10	-1.56	-0.16	1.39	1.38	3.73	3.45	2.58	-1.57	26.73	20.31	6.42
1997	4.67	1.95	4.34	13.15	4.06	5.70	4.01	-0.32	4.92	-2.79	7.75	6.87	68.74	31.39	37.35
1998	4.84	6.62	4.94	6.94	0.60	7.00	1.28	-9.71	7.72	-3.47	5.87	2.53	39.36	27.04	12.32
1999	6.98	4.22	8.66	11.92	10.07	4.62	0.35	5.60	5.11	12.75	9.87	6.47	129.40	19.11	110.29
2000	-4.16	6.82	5.02	1.45	7.94	4.64	9.22	-0.06	4.52	4.83	6.56	3.90	63.12	-10.68	73.80
2001	7.65	6.40	4.60	4.77	6.45	4.05	2.86	4.04	0.47	6.74	0.25	3.55	65.62	-12.87	78.49
2002	4.71	2.70	-0.95	7.71	4.42	1.72	3.12	2.87	1.41	-1.52	4.27	2.08	37.44	-22.81	60.25
2003	-2.70	6.30	2.35	1.64	3.03	15.95	5.60	4.58	9.69	5.76	4.58	4.16	79.40	26.12	53.28
2004	11.15	0.60	-0.56	-0.92	2.67	5.44	-1.83	3.15	6.12	4.15	9.63	7.09	56.70	8.94	47.77
2005	0.90	7.16	5.57	-2.56	7.05	6.23	5.56	0.70	3.66	3.39	8.82	1.26	58.76	3.01	55.74
2006	4.43	-3.65	14.43	1.55	7.77	-4.26	-2.89	-5.04	0.96	4.26	4.64	1.66	24.54	13.74	10.80
2007	4.27	0.25	-0.91	4.02	5.06	4.30	0.65	3.65	5.62	9.52	-0.73	9.10	54.32	3.24	51.08
2008	-0.16	4.69	3.75	0.23	1.57	6.46	6.36	-0.70	3.07	0.04	3.96	4.75	39.37	-38.28	77.66
2009	0.24	-0.18	-0.33	4.39	2.67	-1.82	-0.80	9.10	9.09	4.38	2.56	-0.82	31.54	23.49	8.05
2010	-1.16	4.08	1.24	4.37	-1.50	1.20	-0.39	-1.78	6.31	4.33	1.24	-0.66	18.24	12.84	5.40
2011	-1.41	0.67	5.40	-1.12	4.62	1.44	4.78	-5.01	0.29	5.32	0.70	-0.02	16.19	-0.20	16.39
2012	4.69	3.43	6.21	4.17	4.45	-1.46	0.36	0.64	1.53	-12.87	1.59	0.84	27.12	13.47	13.65
2013	7.81	1.81	4.99	0.59	9.77	-0.60	1.48	2.49	6.78	-1.89	5.30	-0.72	44.07	26.69	14.38
2014	3.40	9.23	2.72	5.71	0.53	2.83	2.58	5.57	-6.88	0.03	6.72	3.47	41.20	11.29	29.91
2015	2.73	-2.53	0.80	-7.08	7.25	2.79	4.70	-1.24	-2.96	1.59	2.61	-4.42	3.36	-0.81	4.18
2016	-8.13	0.63	0.06	-1.90	1.15	9.64	0.62	-1.59	1.34	0.75	6.58	8.91	18.10	9.64	8.46
2017	0.72	-0.59	2.39	-0.50	6.31	-0.71	3.92	3.08	7.32	6.43	-1.57	0.86	30.78	19.38	11.39
2018	8.03	-2.57	-4.34	-1.86	3.78	-1.27	0.64	3.21	4.98	-2.81	-2.65	-2.97	1.36	-6.35	7.70
2019	4.48	2.76	5.75	-4.66	-4.14	3.03	4.49						11.70	20.61	-8.92

The equity curve is smoother, the drawdowns are less severe, and there are far fewer double-digit drawdown months. The compounded annual growth rate has dropped slightly to 39.59 percent, but the maximum drawdown has dropped from 35 percent when two systems are combined to 19.3 percent with three systems.

It's easy to look at that 43 percent growth rate and say you want that, but can you stomach the 35 percent drawdown? There's no use trying to trade it if you can't. If we can smooth out the drawdowns, getting them lower and lower while only paying a small price in CAGR performance, then you end up with a superior system you're more likely to trade. Once you've done that, if you want to shoot for the moon you have a lot more possibilities with position sizing to actually have an algorithm that achieves your objectives.

It's easier to size a system that has a MAR of 3.0 than a MAR of 0.7. With a higher MAR, you trade more comfortably. We want to make sure you do not abandon your system. If you have a 25 percent drawdown and you can't handle it, you abandon your system at the worst time. If you have a system that only has 10 percent drops, you're likely to be a lot more comfortable trading it. Consistency is one of the most important parts of successful trading.

Chart 20: Suite vs. Benchmark Volatility

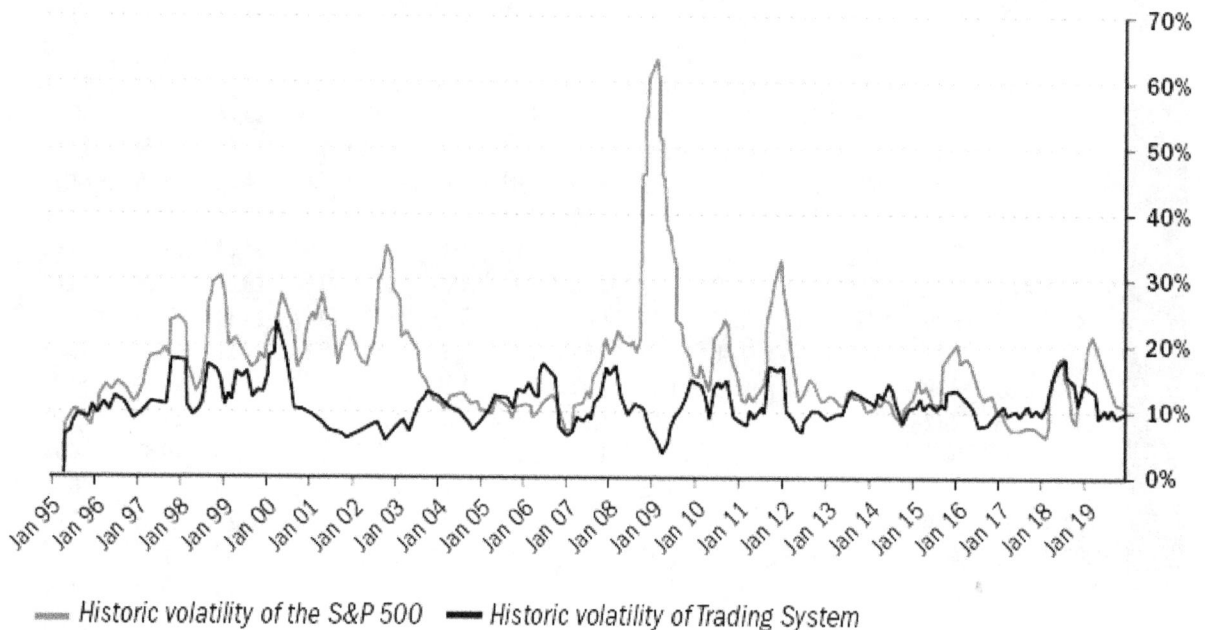

===== Historic volatility of the S&P 500 ▬▬ Historic volatility of Trading System

Also take a look at this chart where we combine the historic volatility of the benchmark, the S&P 500 versus our system, which now is a combination of one trend following long, one mean reversion long and one mean reversion short. Imagine being in those huge volatile times like 2008 only trading long. You'd have a volatility in your portfolio that at its peak was six times higher than this system.

It is one of the key benefits of combining noncorrelating systems that it lowers the volatility but increases the CAGR and lowers the drawdowns.

As we add systems, we are improving the performance of the combined system. The number of systems is not the key to success; it's the fact that they are not correlated. If you were to add a second trend following system that loses money at exactly the same time as Long Trend High Momentum, that does not add any real value.

However, sometimes noncorrelated systems become correlated. If there is a big market selloff, long systems will all correlate. Most of the time, there is not a big selloff, of course, and we can find huge noncorrelation edges in the corporate risk of individual stocks. And when the long systems do, in fact, become closely correlated, we have short-selling systems to compensate for that.

Every system makes money in certain markets and loses money in certain markets. If you can spread those good and bad moments out, your equity curve gets a lot smoother.

Chapter 8

How and Why Trading More Systems Simultaneously Improves Returns

Up to now we have been exploring how combining investment systems with different styles and different directions results in a higher risk-adjusted return. The question is, can we continue to expand on that, or does adding more styles create overlaps and redundancies that don't help so much?

Even before we answer that question, let's consider a more fundamental query: Why would we want to add more systems? After all, the three systems we have in place give us a backtested result of 39 percent CAGR and a 19 percent maximum drawdown. That's pretty good performance!

To answer this question we should consider the following factors:

1. **Corporate risk**

2. **Temporary nonperformance of systems. (variability of returns of single systems)**

3. **Scalability**

4. **Lower volatility of the overall equity curve**

Corporate risk is associated with a corporate event.

This includes earning warnings, a bankruptcy, the CEO resigning or falling ill, there are charges of insider fraud or a change in dividend policy (higher or lower—if you're shorting the stock, a higher dividend isn't likely to help you), and so on. Events like these can move a stock in ways that do not correlate to the market. The moves can be sudden and dramatic. A CEO can step down one evening after trading closes and the next day the stock can open 10 percent lower.

If we have a big position in the stock, that surprise can really affect performance—positively or negatively, depending on the news and our position. So while you can find an edge here, if you suddenly have several corporate events, that's going to affect your portfolio in ways you have not foreseen.

Imagine being long in a stock that is trading at $2.70. After the markets close, the company issues a profit warning. The next day the stock opens at $0.40. Even if you have a 20 percent trailing stop, it doesn't matter, the stock gapped down over your stop-loss. That exact situation happened to me. It's a situation that, sooner or later, will happen to everybody. It does not matter that this scenario does not show up in your backtest. I promise: eventually, it *will* happen. I have traded long enough to tell you this is a guarantee. When the move is in your favor you tend not to pay too much attention to it—in fact, you feel cool because you made a great profit.

Chart 21: ANTH Feb 9 - March 8, 2018

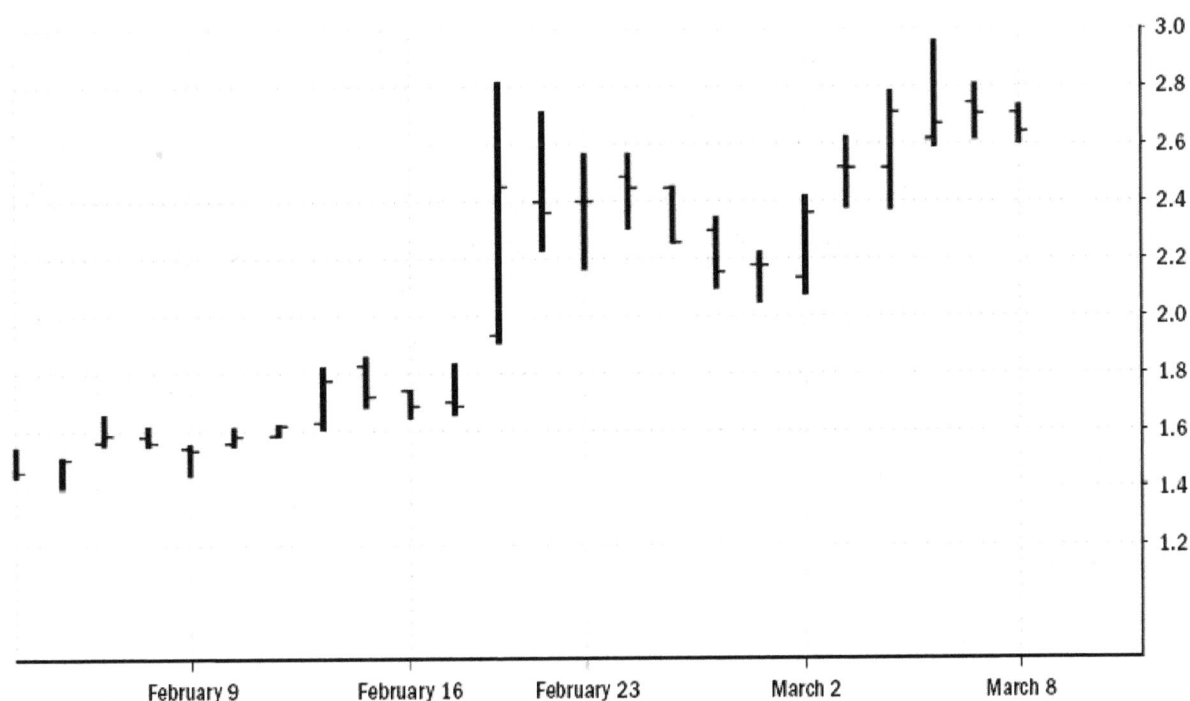

Chart 22: ANTH March 9, 2018

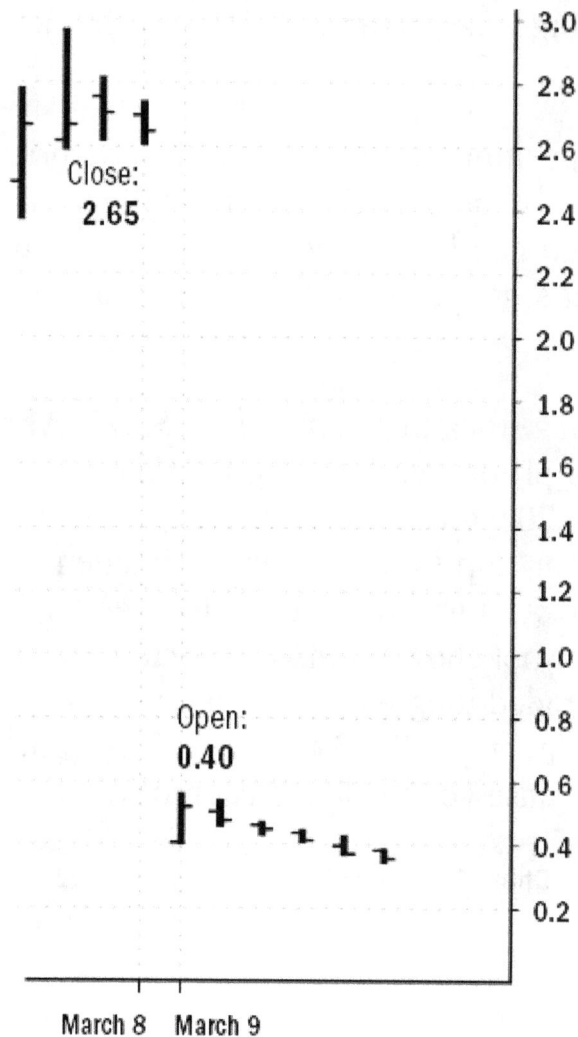

Or imagine you are short in a biotech stock that is trading at $2.00. After hours, the company issues a press release indicating it has had a patent approved. The next day the stock opens at $4.00. (This sort of thing is common with very volatile stocks like biotechs.) If you are in too large of a position on the wrong side of a trade, it can wipe you out. Your stop-loss price doesn't matter; the stop will be executed at the open price, but it has lost its protective function.

See real-life examples here:

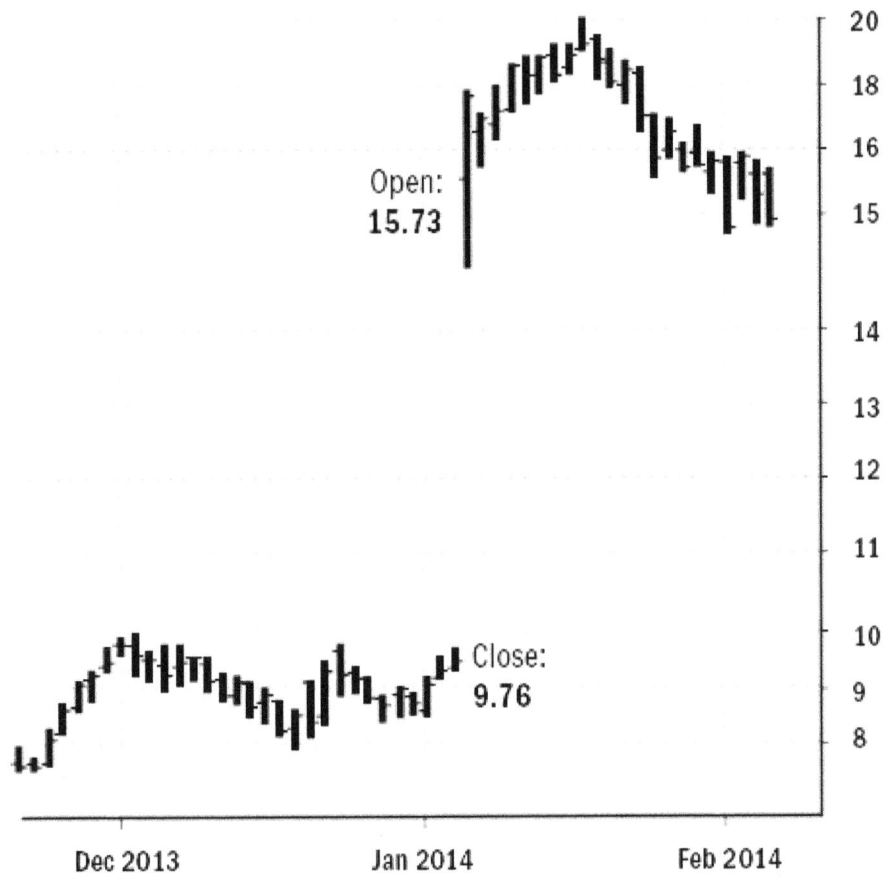

Chart 23: NBIX – Gapping Up

Open: 15.73

Close: 9.76

Chart 24: ICPT – Gapping Up

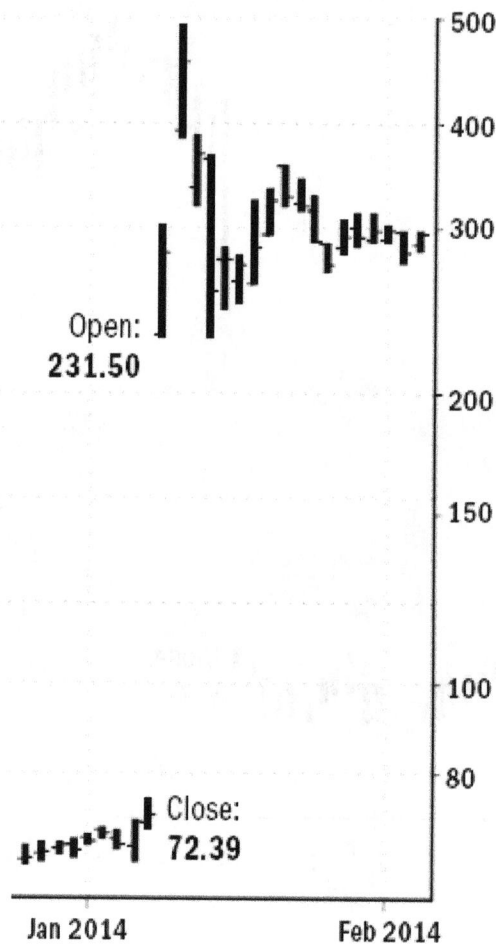

In both of these examples, if you had been short, the losses the day after would have been huge. The larger your position the larger the losses. Therefore, we must be careful with corporate events. They *can* move in your favor, in which case you will feel like a genius, but if you are at the wrong side and you have a too large percentage of your equity allocated to this stock it can wipe you out.

The way to protect yourself from corporate risk is to allocate less money to each position. And the way to do that is to have more systems, and thus more positions, for your equity. The more systems you have, the lower the impact of any corporate event on your equity. If you trade one system with 10 percent of your equity in each position, the negative impact is twice as high as if you trade two systems with 5 percent of your equity in each position. (This assumes you make sure only to take a single directional position in a company across your systems. For example, you don't want to be long in the same stock in two different systems, although you could be long in one system and short in another.)

Temporary Nonperformance **can and will happen to any system**

Every single system will face conditions where it simply doesn't make money (as it should). That's part of life and part of trading, and you have to deal with it. The result can be a longer than expected bad performance streak. This means the system at times will perform worse than your backtest. That does not mean there is something wrong with it; it is just random behavior. Nonperformance can happen even if you are long in a bull market, but you happen to have positions in a couple of stocks that simply underperform. That will pull the whole system performance down.

Take a look here at the rolling returns of one of the trend following systems. Rolling returns is a simple calculation where we look each day back at what the net performance has been of the system over the chosen timeframe.

Table 19: 12-Month Rolling Returns, Trend Following System

January 2, 1995 – July 24, 2019	Trading System
CAGR%	22.52%
Max 12-Month Return	142.75%
Min 12-Month Return	-28.56%

Although we see that the CAGR is 22.52 percent over the last twenty-four years, these results do not come equally every year. There has been a period of twelve months where the return was more than 124 percent, but also there was a time where the return over twelve months was -28 percent.

Chart 25: 12-Month Rolling Returns, Trend Following System

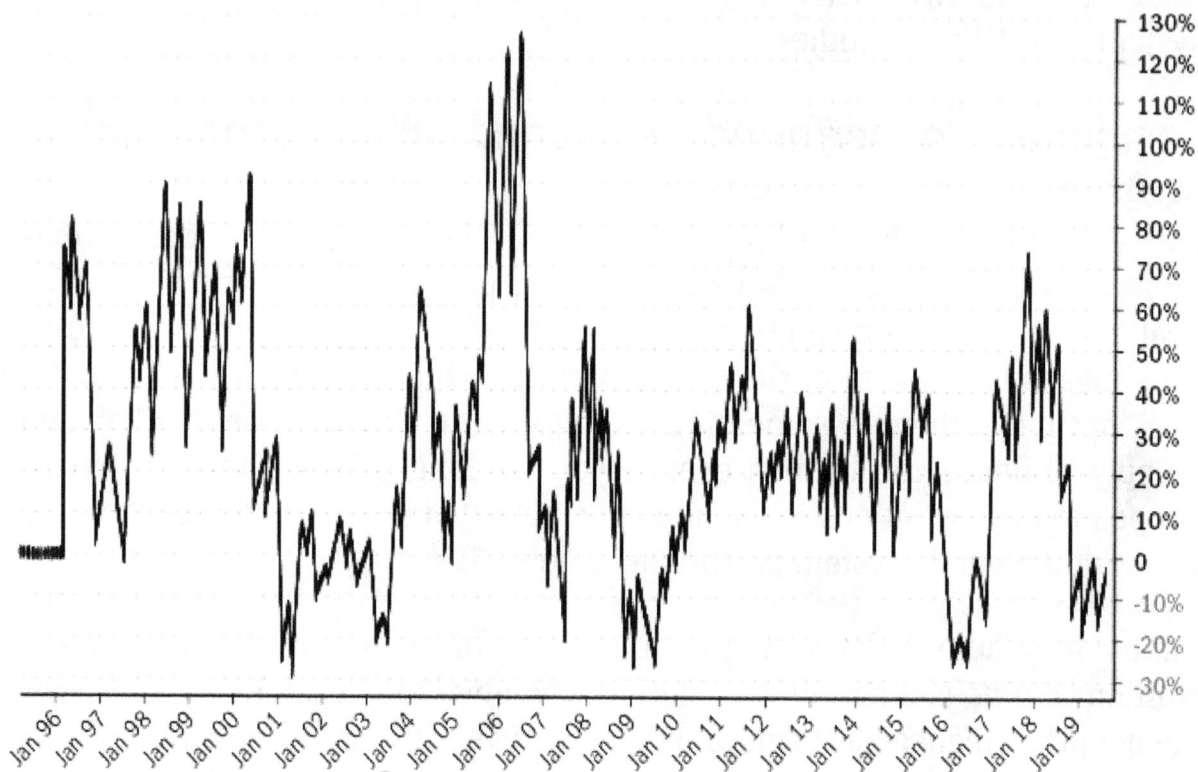

As clearly illustrated in this chart, there are times when the system creates great wealth and other times when it does not.

If you are able to create different systems with different entry, ranking, and exit logic so you have totally noncorrelating systems, then this variability of results will happen at different times and thus when combined, create a smoother equity curve with lower volatility. The drawdowns won't be so deep and the risk adjusted return is higher.

You might be saying to yourself, "wait a minute, if I cut my downside in half, don't I also cut my upside in half?" This is the magic of multiple noncorrelated systems! Because different systems make money at different times, and each system is designed to have a better than average statistical edge, you get more upside performance by having more systems in place. You reduce the downward drag on results while adding in upward effects to your CAGR, producing a smoother equity curve.

Combining more and more noncorrelating systems also reduces the overall volatility of the portfolio, even as risk-adjusted return increases. Additional systems smooth the equity curve by diminishing the effect (positive or negative) of any single system, while simultaneously adding in more trading edges that accumulate on the positive side of the performance ledger. With a higher risk-adjusted return, we can be more aggressive with position sizing to achieve our goals.

Remember, when we trade multiple systems in different directions, market direction becomes irrelevant. We can profit in all market types if we have built enough systems to anticipate all market types. If you trade one long system, and it doesn't perform for some random reason (for example, you are in stocks that didn't do as well as expected), you miss out on the big run-up. If you trade five long systems in a bull market, and one of them isn't performing, that nonperforming system isn't going to make a big difference to your portfolio. And, of course, if you trade long and short at the same time, then you are going to capture value no matter which way the market moves, which is incredibly important for your mental state.

Scalability

Another benefit of trading multiple systems comes when you build up a sizable account. If you only trade a few systems, you may find that your positions become so large in dollar terms that you can't trade them—you might move the market enough to erode your edge. This is why larger funds cannot trade in stocks with smaller volumes.

Also, since we are trading short, there is only a certain quantity of shares available to short. If our positions are too big, the broker will not have enough shares available.

We again can solve this by trading different stocks in multiple systems and thus allocating less money to each stock, which is key to scale the systems.

Lower volatility of the equity curve

The more noncorrelated systems we trade simultaneously the lower the volatility of returns will be and the smoother the equity curve. The chart below illustrates this perfectly:

Chart 26: Equity Curve by System

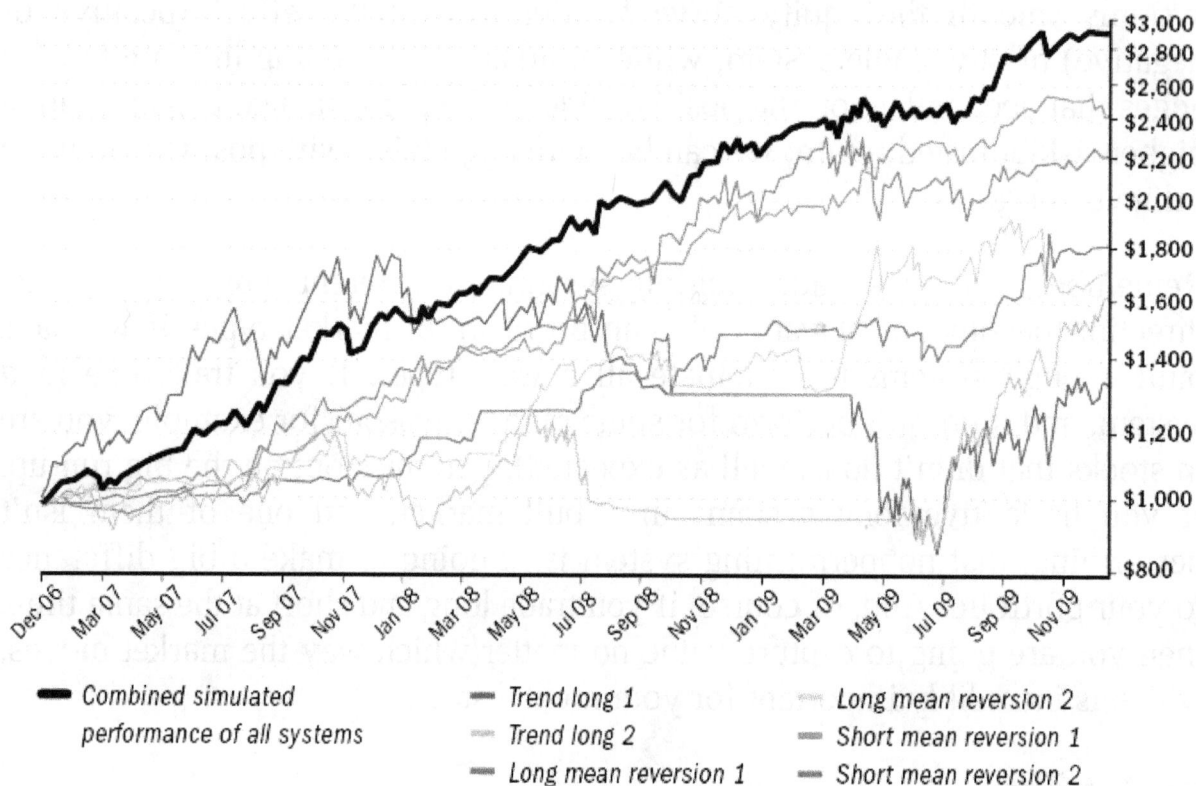

Legend:
- **Combined simulated performance of all systems** (black)
- Trend long 1
- Trend long 2
- Long mean reversion 1
- Long mean reversion 2
- Short mean reversion 1
- Short mean reversion 2

Compare the equity curve of the individual systems to the performance of the suite as a whole. Notice how much less volatile the overall performance is. In the slide above, the black line represents the combined equity of the systems. You can see that some of the long systems went flat—to cash—during the 2008–2009 period, yet the overall system continued to make money because the short systems kicked in. Again, look at how much less volatile the suite as a whole is.

Chapter 9

Expanding the Number of Noncorrelated Systems

Systems 4, 5, and 6

In this chapter I'll show you how to bring in three more systems that most of the time don't correlate with the three we've already discussed. The more noncorrelated systems you have—and noncorrelation is the key—the more consistent your returns will be, regardless of market behavior.

How to Expand Your Number of Systems

We bring in additional noncorrelated systems by building new trading systems that employ different entry criteria, rankings, and exits.

You already know that there are two directional positions we can take in a market—long and short—and we use two approaches, mean reversion and trend following. That might seem limiting, but the US markets have a tradable universe of approximately 7,000 stocks to work with. (The exact amount depends a little on your requirement for a stock's liquidity.) This gives us the opportunity to create many different systems to get into different stocks at the right time to make money by creating different buy-and-sell rules.

Let's say we want to build more systems without falling into a trap of having them replicate each other's performance. How can we do that?

Take a trend following system as an example. The first parameter we can adjust is entry. What kind of stocks do we want to be in? In the first long-term trend following system that I described earlier in this book, Long Trend

High Momentum, we specified that we wanted to filter in favor of highly volatile stocks. For a conceptually different system, we can filter for low volatility stocks, which will behave differently. We will have different candidates to trade, and the results will be different. That alone is a big differentiator.

We can also split the market based on volume and pricing. If you build a system to trade stocks that are priced below $10, you will be up against very different market participants, and see very different behaviors, than if you trade more expensive stocks. The same thing is true for low volume and high-volume stocks and, as I mentioned, for more and less volatile stocks.

Knowing that we're in high-momentum stocks in this example, we now use simple trend filters. One way to look for different stocks is to use lookbacks of different durations. We may seek stocks that are above the 50-day simple moving average, or the 100-day, or the 200-day. These indicators show short-, medium- and longer-term uptrends.

Then we can combine with filters that look at pullbacks—for example, a three-day RSI below ten shows a strong pullback; below thirty a medium pullback, below fifty a weak pullback. These pullbacks again give us a larger chance to be in different stocks than a system without a pullback.

Even employing these variables as filters, we might still end up in the same stocks. Next we focus on ranking, which is a very important part of a system. We can rank stocks by highest or lowest historic volatility; most overbought or oversold; and strongest versus weakest trend. You're almost certain to get into different stocks using different rankings.

One last tool for making sure the systems are different is exits. The market can cause systems to be correlated, however, so we want to be sure we have different exit systems. Sometimes when the market drops some systems will be stopped out, but others won't, and then the market recovers again. You can set different sizes and types of profit target (average true range or percent return, for example). You also can have trailing stops of different sizes.

Finally, for a mean reversion system you can vary your days-in-trade limits so no two systems exit the same way.

With this many variables to work with, you can see how you could easily build multiple trading systems that work together in an additive fashion, yet generally don't correlate in negative ways. Doing this will smooth your equity curve and reduce your risk.

Let's take a look at the next three systems:

System 4: Long Trend Low Volatility

- **Objective:** System 1, Long Trend High Momentum, was a high volatility system. Conceptually, you don't want to replicate an existing system, so low volatility is the differentiator here. We already have a system that follows high-volatility stocks, so we'll look for stocks with lower volatility and a different entry rule. We follow trends, but we will actually have a low correlation with the high-volatility LTTF system.
- **Beliefs:** Implicit in this system is the belief that there is great money to be made in lower volatility stocks. They're often held by institutions and represent bigger, stronger companies. Generally, such companies have a more consistent way of managing profit and loss. Their news events tend to be less dramatic and everything tends to run relatively smoothly. We believe there is an opportunity for a more consistent, smooth run-up with these stocks.
- **Trading universe:** All stocks on the NASDAQ, NYSE, and AMEX.
- **Filter:**
  - Average daily dollar volume greater than $100 million over the last fifty days.
  - Historic volatility rating between 10 and 40 percent, which puts us in the lower range on that metric.
- **Setup:**
  - Close of the S&P 500 is above 200-day simple moving average. This means the index is in an uptrend.
  - Close of the stock is above the 200-day. simple moving average.
- **Ranking:** Lowest four-day RSI, which means ranking by the stocks that are the most oversold. This is another distinction from our first trend following system, where we were ranking by the highest rate of change. Here we're looking for the most oversold.
- **Entry:** Market on open. We want to be sure to get into the trade

regardless of slippage.

- **Stop-Loss:** The day after execution, we place a stop-loss of one-and-a-half times the average true range (ATR) of the last forty days below the execution price. This is quite a small stop-loss. What we are doing is risking a small amount and getting a huge asymmetric return when a stock moves in our favor.
- **Reentry:** Yes
- **Profit Protection:** We also place a trailing stop of 20 percent. This allows us to protect gains as the stock continues to rise.
- **Profit Taking:** None. We let trend following winners run.
- **Position Sizing:** 2 percent risk and 10 percent maximum percent size.

Table 20: Results for Long Trend Low Volatility

January 2, 1995 – July 24, 2019	Trading System
CAGR%	13.37%
Maximum Drawdown	21.13%
Annualized Volatility	14.80%
Sharpe	0.90
MAR	0.63
Win%	29.62%
Win/Loss	6.41
Total Return	2,077.88%

Chart 27: Equity Curve for Long Trend Low Volatility

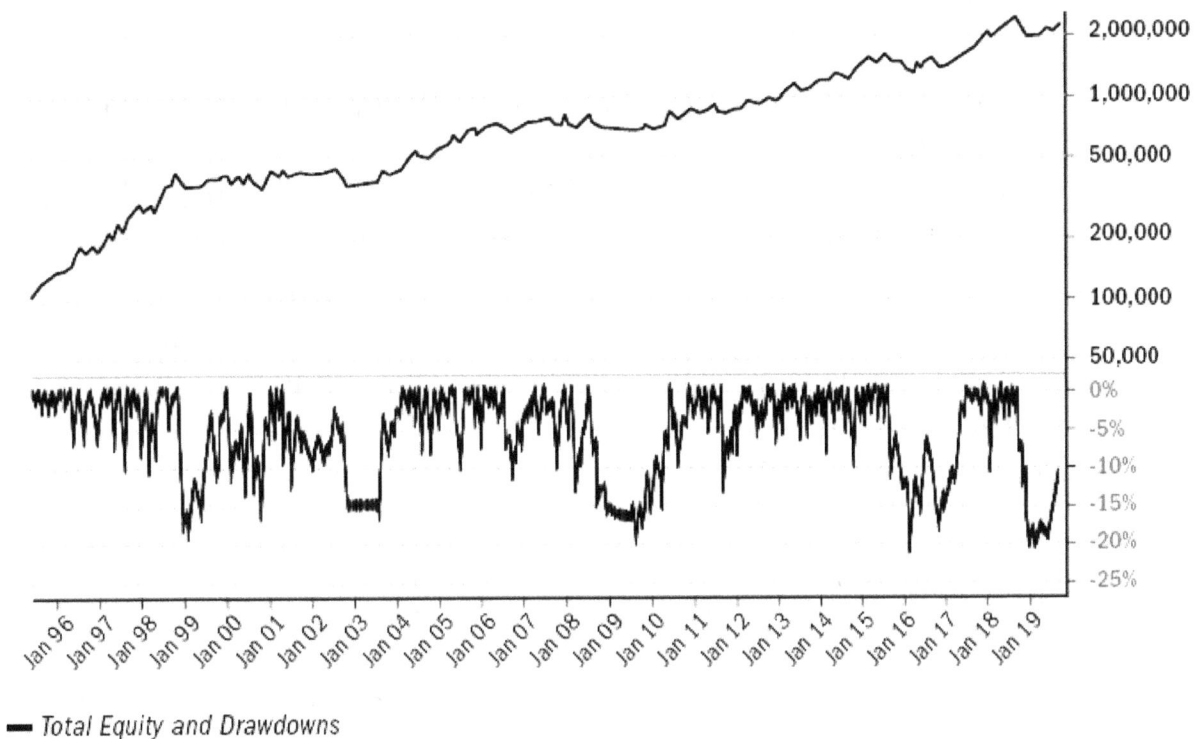

— *Total Equity and Drawdowns*

You can see the return is 13.3 percent, but the maximum drawdown is only 21.1 percent, which is good, and the longest drawdown is thirty-four months, also good for trend following. The most interesting thing about this system is the win rate is only 29.6 percent; the Win/Loss ratio is 6.4:1, so the trades that win do quite well. **This is a classic example of an asymmetric trading system. You can lose a small amount repeatedly, but every now and then you get those huge winners that make up for all the losses.**

People who trade this as a single system can grow uncomfortable with that low win rate. This is a system that depends on our core principle of cutting losses and letting winners keep going until they stop.

System 5: Long Mean Reversion High ADX Reversal

- **Objective:** To buy stocks that are in an uptrend, have a significant selloff (which is our buy point), and revert to their mean. This system must be different than Mean Reversion Selloff.
- **Beliefs**: After a selloff the stock will revert to its mean and continue the uptrend.

- **Trading Universe:** All stocks traded on the NYSE, AMEX, and NASDAQ.
- **Filter:**
    - Average daily volume over the last fifty trading days of at least 500,000 shares
    - Average dollar volume of at least $2.5 million over the last fifty trading days. These two filters combined ensure that if we trade low-priced stocks, we will have sufficient volume.
    - ATR greater than 4 percent. We want to trade volatile stocks because this is a mean reversion system and is only in the stock for a few days.
- **Setup:**
    - Close above 100-day SMA plus one ATR of the last ten days. This measures a more significant uptrend.
    - Seven-day ADX is greater than fifty-five, showing good strength of movement.
    - Three-day RSI is less than fifty. This indicates a moderate pullback.
- **Ranking:** Highest seven-day ADX.
- **Entry:** Buy limit 3 percent below previous close. We are looking for slightly oversold stocks in big uptrends; by buying at 3 percent below the close, we're setting up a big edge to capture a bounce back toward the mean. With a system like this you will not always have a full portfolio, because not all stocks will drop another 3 percent. You might place ten orders and only execute three or four of them.
- **Stop-Loss:** Three ATR of the last ten days below the execution price. This is a wide stop-loss, but we need room for the stock to drop lower before it reverts. We don't want to be stopped out before the stock reverts to the mean.
- **Reentry:** Yes
- **Profit Protection:** None
- **Profit Taking:**
    - One ATR of the last ten days, then sell next day market on open
    - Time-based: After six trading days, if not stopped out and the profit target is not hit, then exit next day market on open.
- **Position Sizing:** 2 percent risk and 10 percent maximum percent size.

Table 21: Results for Long Mean Reversion High ADX Reversal

January 2, 1995 – July 24, 2019	Trading System
CAGR%	17.24%
Maximum Drawdown	17.39%
Annualized Volatility	12.66%
Sharpe	1.36
MAR	0.99
Win%	57.52%
Win/Loss	0.97
Total Return	4,863.33%

Chart 28: Equity Curve for Long Mean Reversion High ADX Reversal

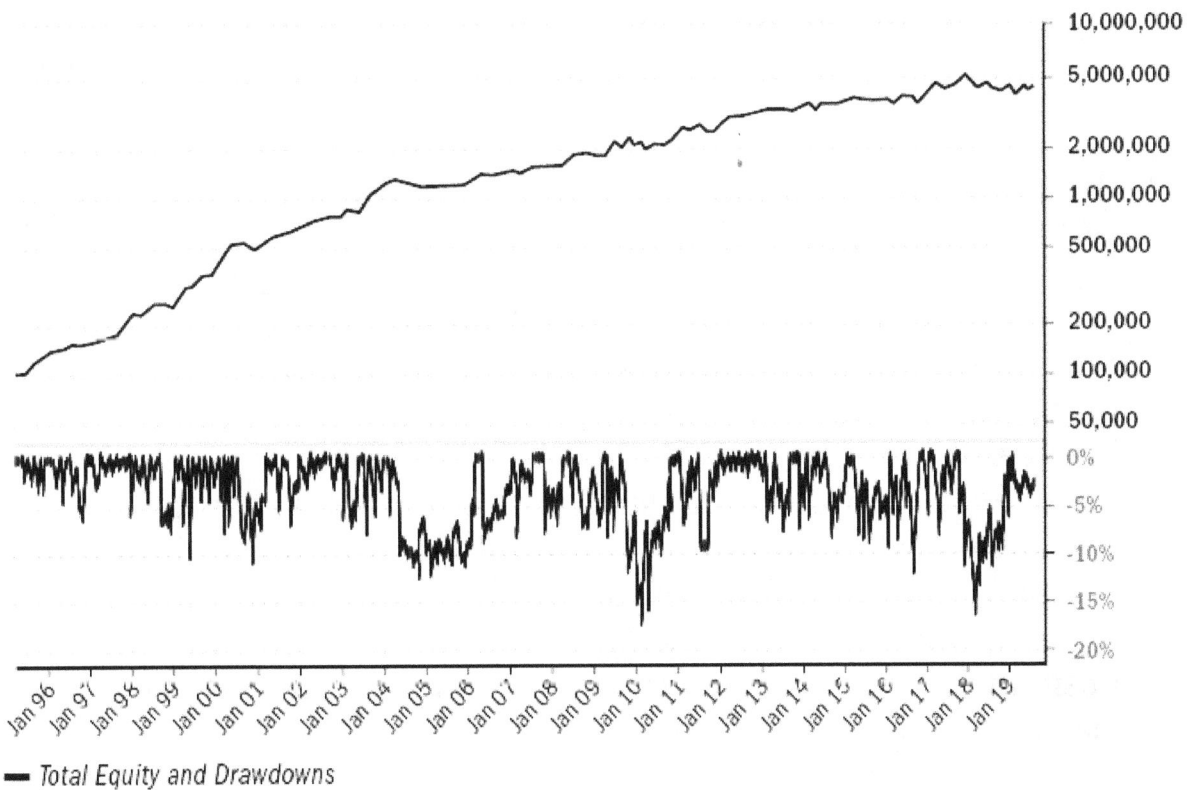

— *Total Equity and Drawdowns*

You can see the mean reversion systems tend to have a lower drawdown than trend following systems. This system has a CAGR of 17.24 and a maximum drawdown of 17.4 percent, resulting in a MAR of 0.99.

System 6: Short Mean Reversion High Six-Day Surge

- **Objective:** A second mean reversion short system that does not overlap with Short RSI Thrust, seeking profit from overbought stocks. This system might lose money in bull markets but can do very well in sideways and down markets.
- **Beliefs:** An extended price increase of the stock means there is a large chance of it correcting and reverting back to its mean.
- **Trading Universe:** All stocks on the NYSE, AMEX, and NASDAQ.
- **Filter:**
  - Minimum price $5
  - Average dollar volume $10 million over the last fifty trading days.
- **Setup:**
  - The price of the stock has increased at least 20 percent over the last six trading days.
  - Last two days had positive closes. These two indicators mean the stock is very popular; there has been a lot of buying pressure.
- **Ranking:** Biggest six-day price increase.
- **Entry:** Sell limit 5 percent above the previous close. This creates a big edge; we are looking for the stock to go 5 percent higher in intra-day trading before we short it.
- **Stop-Loss:** Three ATR of the last ten trading days above the execution price.
- **Reentry:** Yes
- **Profit Protection:** None, because of the short trade duration.
- **Profit Taking:**
  - 5 percent, then exit next day market on close
  - Or time-based exit after three days of market on close
- **Position Sizing:** 2 percent risk of equity in the trade, and a 10 percent maximum of system equity involved any single trade.

Table 22: Results for Short Mean Reversion High Six-Day Surge

January 2, 1995 – July 24, 2019	Trading System
CAGR%	19.27%
Maximum Drawdown	32.40%
Annualized Volatility	14.18%
Sharpe	1.36
MAR	0.59
Win%	60.92%
Win/Loss	0.59
Total Return	7,480.28%

Chart 29: Equity Curve for Short Mean Reversion High Six-Day Surge

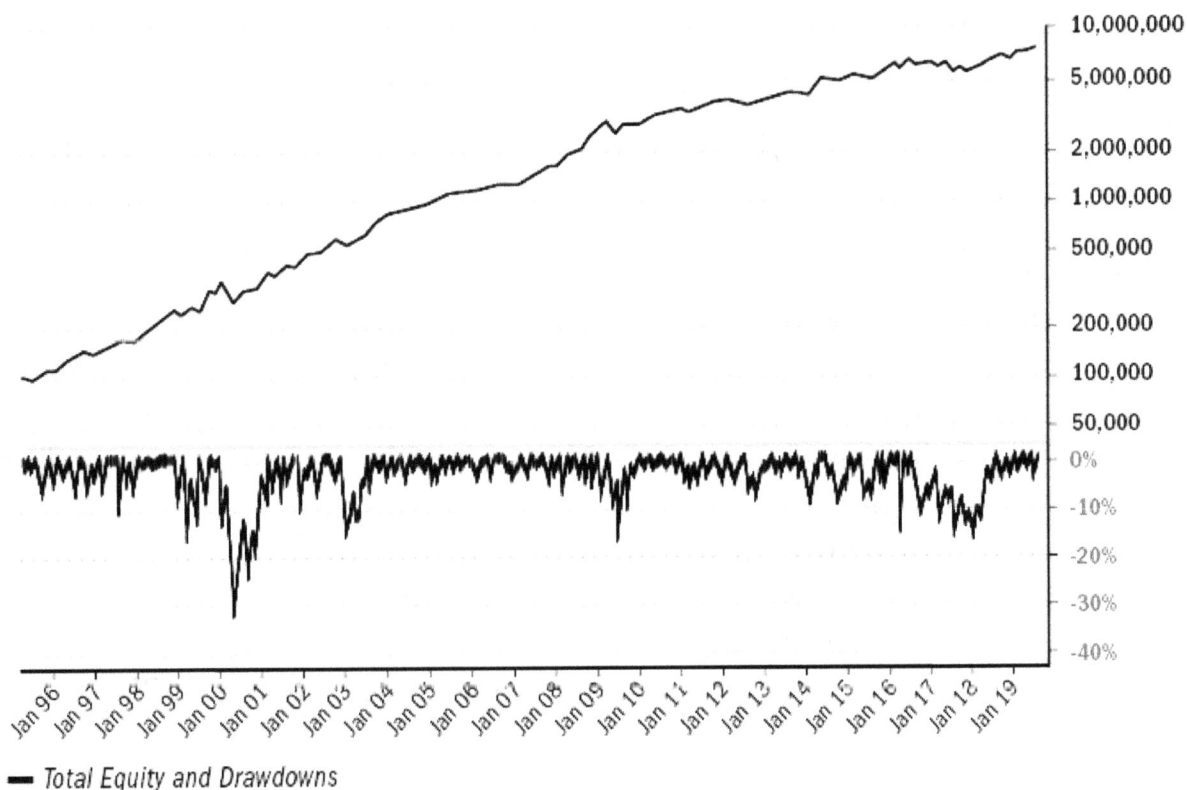

— Total Equity and Drawdowns

This system has a solid growth rate of 19 percent. You see a larger drawdown than the previous system, at 32 percent. That's not a cause for concern, because when this system is losing money, your bull market systems are making money. Notice how in the peak of the dot-com bull market in 2000, when all long systems made big money, it had its biggest drawdown, but in 2008–2009 it made a lot of money.

A note of caution

As you bring in more systems, beware of the risk of the systems lockstepping during extreme market events. By this I mean the following:

You may build several systems that trade in the same direction and the same style, such as trend following long. They may be noncorrelated during bull and sideways markets, making and losing money at different times and creating an overall profitable scenario for you. However, during major selloffs, such systems can become correlated—they can all go down together. Don't think that developing multiple long systems protects you. You must add in systems that trade short.

Putting It All Together

These charts below show the combined results of all six systems, traded 100 percent long and 100 percent short simultaneously, so that on any given day we can never be more than 100 percent long and 100 percent short.:

- Four long systems
    - Two trend-following
        - System 1: Long Trend High Momentum (25 percent of trading capital)
        - System 4: Long Trend Low Volatility (25 percent of trading capital)
    - Two mean reversion
        - System 3: Long Mean Reversion Selloff (25 percent of trading capital)
        - System 5: Long Mean Reversion ADX Reversal (25 percent of trading capital)
- Two short systems
    - System 2: Short RSI Thrust (50 percent of trading capital)
    - System 6: Short Mean Reversion High Six-Day Surge (50

percent of trading capital)

Table 23: Results for Six Systems Combined

January 2, 1995 – July 24, 2019	Trading System	SPY
CAGR%	35.30%	8.02%
Maximum Drawdown	11.30%	56.47%
Annualized Volatility	12.18%	18.67%
Sharpe	2.90	0.43
MAR	3.12	0.14
Daily Return Correlation to Benchmark	0.26	NA
Total Return	167,592.19%	562.51%

Chart 30: Equity Curve for Six Systems Combined

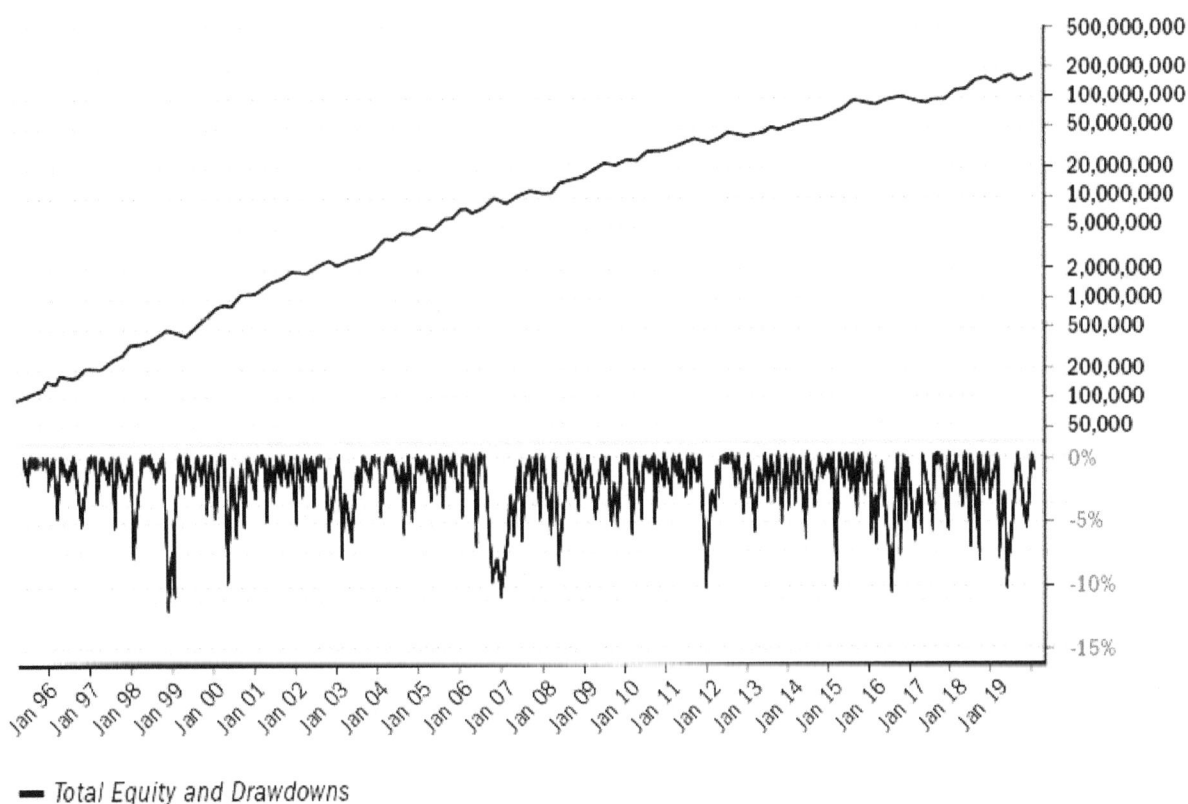

— Total Equity and Drawdowns

Remember that between 1995 and 2019 our benchmark, the S&P 500, delivered a CAGR of 8 percent, with a maximum drawdown of 56 percent, a longest drawdown of eighty-six months.

By comparison, our six combined, noncorrelated systems delivered a CAGR of 35 percent, an 11 percent maximum drawdown, and a longest drawdown of eleven months. Volatility is two-thirds that of the benchmark.

These results are the eighth wonder of the world. It's incredible how well noncorrelated systems work together to smooth the equity curve and delivery consistent results regardless of market conditions.

Chart 31: Equity Curves for Six Systems and Combined Suite

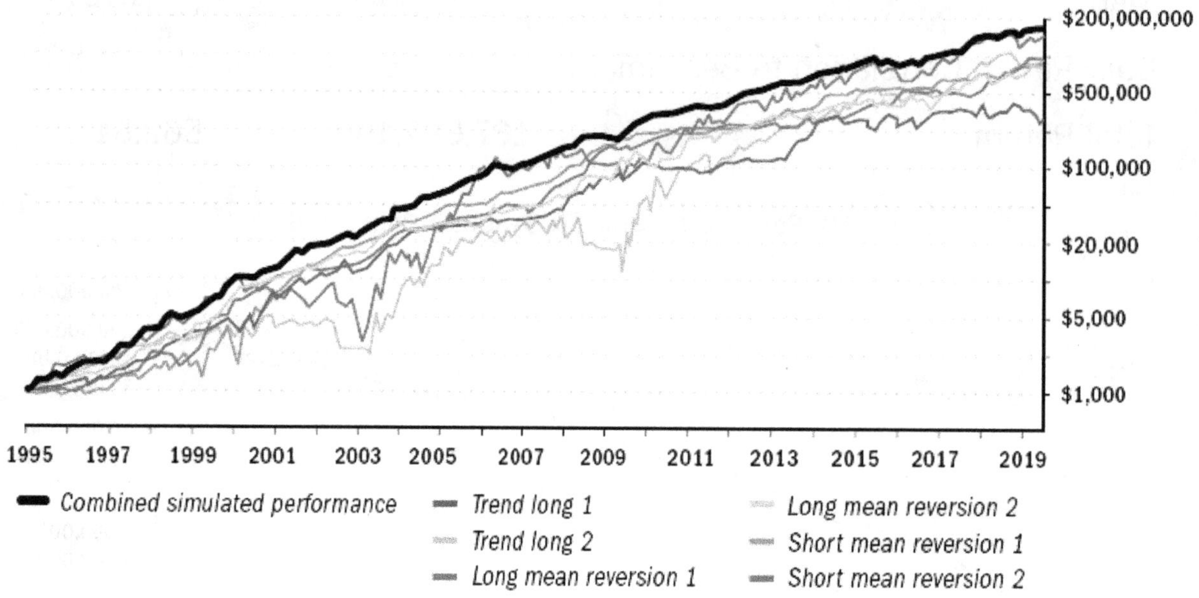

$200,000,000
$500,000
$100,000
$20,000
$5,000
$1,000
1995
1997
1999
2001
2003
2005
2007
2009
2011
2013
2015
2017
2019
Combined simulated performance
Trend long 1
Trend long 2
Long mean reversion 1
Long mean reversion 2
Short mean reversion 1
Short mean reversion 2

Table 24: Combined Monthly Results for Six Systems

%	JAN	FEB	MAR	APR	MAY	JUN	JUL	AUG	SEP	OCT	NOV	DEC	ANNUAL	SPY	COMPARISON
1995	1.34	1.19	5.17	0.52	5.57	4.67	2.65	5.36	10.33	-2.29	4.60	1.51	**48.28**	35.16	**13.12**
1996	2.81	5.54	2.96	2.62	1.69	0.49	-0.08	-1.16	4.55	4.38	2.22	0.84	**30.14**	20.31	**9.82**
1997	7.43	3.47	3.12	9.88	1.96	8.57	5.22	1.69	4.62	0.58	5.75	4.45	**73.38**	31.39	**42.00**
1998	2.52	7.53	4.28	9.60	1.01	6.03	0.27	-7.56	6.50	-2.58	4.31	4.71	**41.76**	27.04	**14.72**
1999	7.07	6.04	4.94	8.54	7.07	3.41	4.68	8.11	1.79	5.46	2.89	2.57	**83.58**	19.11	**64.47**
2000	-2.44	4.60	8.45	2.95	7.25	-3.22	3.92	1.24	6.07	7.17	6.49	7.39	**61.73**	-10.68	**72.41**
2001	0.59	6.40	3.63	4.12	5.15	0.52	4.46	1.74	-1.09	3.10	2.42	3.70	**40.49**	-12.87	**53.36**
2002	3.66	3.04	1.52	4.08	3.57	1.65	1.18	2.65	0.59	-3.35	-0.05	1.20	**21.36**	-22.81	**44.17**
2003	-0.15	2.80	4.17	2.15	7.22	14.02	5.09	4.03	6.45	3.11	5.91	5.06	**78.32**	26.12	**52.20**
2004	7.72	2.07	-0.27	-1.54	1.17	3.38	-1.17	2.70	3.10	2.92	7.41	2.55	**33.58**	8.94	**24.64**
2005	0.83	8.34	3.62	-1.32	5.64	4.10	3.82	0.38	3.09	1.50	6.04	1.05	**42.13**	3.01	**39.12**
2006	4.31	-1.13	7.26	3.21	6.01	-2.20	-1.78	-0.05	-0.79	1.81	2.48	0.80	**21.23**	13.74	**7.49**
2007	3.46	-1.60	-0.86	5.63	3.51	0.94	-0.01	8.56	4.99	8.48	-1.36	8.47	**47.37**	3.24	**44.13**
2008	-3.38	5.80	1.93	2.72	3.63	4.58	6.49	1.63	2.73	1.67	3.50	4.85	**42.28**	-38.28	**80.56**
2009	2.41	1.06	0.80	5.58	0.16	-1.56	0.75	3.68	7.39	0.50	1.44	2.41	**26.85**	23.49	**3.53**
2010	-1.45	3.55	2.55	5.76	-1.89	1.33	3.02	-1.55	6.18	3.52	2.44	0.53	**26.32**	12.84	**13.48**
2011	-0.37	1.96	2.00	-0.78	3.26	1.21	2.15	-4.26	0.41	5.23	1.96	1.67	**15.08**	-0.20	**15.28**
2012	2.46	2.90	3.72	2.20	2.23	-1.80	-0.20	0.79	3.28	-0.90	1.94	0.24	**18.04**	13.47	**4.57**
2013	5.76	0.65	1.25	1.62	8.82	-1.88	1.80	0.67	4.84	1.94	4.21	-3.09	**29.40**	26.69	**-0.29**
2014	-0.04	8.79	5.13	3.83	1.00	1.28	0.37	3.20	-4.33	1.15	5.12	4.73	**34.00**	11.29	**22.71**
2015	1.92	1.42	2.86	-3.73	4.28	0.71	2.10	0.11	-2.01	0.48	3.00	-0.20	**11.23**	-0.81	**12.04**
2016	-3.88	0.54	3.70	-0.36	-1.38	6.16	-0.53	-3.57	0.97	-0.38	5.53	5.79	**12.59**	9.64	**2.94**
2017	1.29	-1.02	4.32	0.88	3.90	-2.36	1.89	4.28	4.78	6.05	2.31	0.38	**29.81**	19.38	**10.42**
2018	8.64	-2.91	-2.36	0.99	6.05	0.24	2.62	2.85	4.08	-5.95	2.26	-2.26	**14.18**	-6.35	**20.53**
2019	2.51	3.42	6.00	-2.31	-2.44	2.98	5.05						**15.85**	20.61	**-4.76**

These graphs together show how consistent returns now are. There is a preponderance of positive-return months, and the worst return was 7.56 percent in August 1998. This is another representation of smoothing the equity curve. The combined systems dampen the equity curve's volatility, which is great in down years, but in big bull years means the system may not beat the index.

Chapter 10

The Risk of the Unknown

System 7

Even though we have a backtesting data sample spanning twenty-four years, that does not mean that we have a perfect representation of what may happen in the future! It is perfect from the past and very robust. But it doesn't incorporate scenarios we have seen in the past and know can happen, such as the 1929 crash or the 1987 crash.

Imagine you start trading and the following happens:

Chart 32: S&P 500 Index: 1929 – 1932 Depression -86%

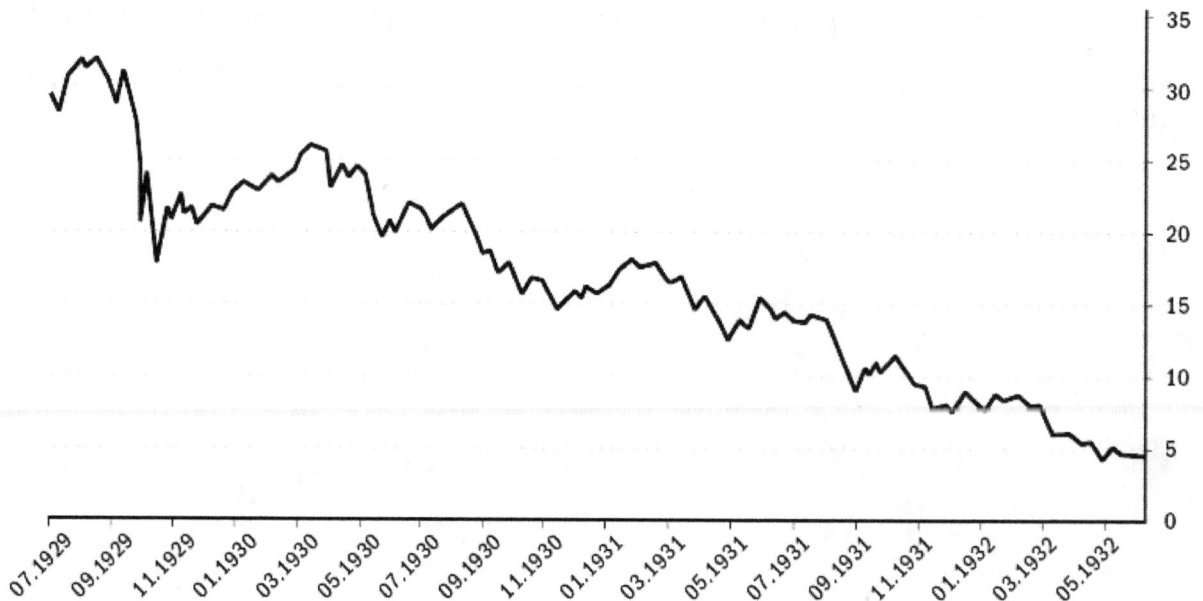

Or this happens:

Chart 33: S&P 500 Inflationary Era: 1968 – 1982
(not adjusted for inflation)

Or you run into this:

Chart 34: S&P 500: 1987 Crash

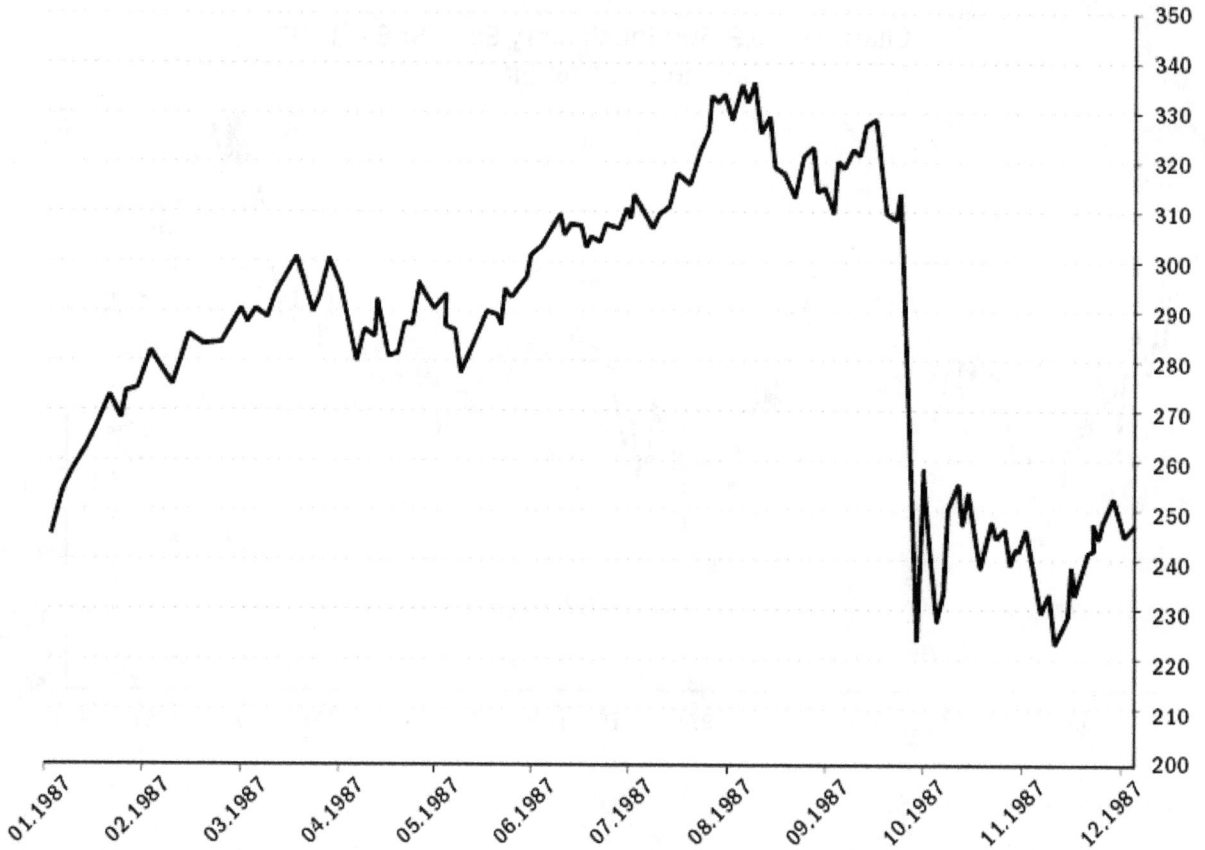

Do the graphs above look anything like our backtest sample?

Chart 35: S&P 500: 1995 – 2019: Our sample size

Obviously, they do not. We have only been able to backtest on a sample that represents a fairly bullish market. The future might look very different. Therefore, we need to think conceptually about what could happen.

Although we trade short-selling systems to protect us during downturns, they have some risks:

- One risk is that the government might ban the short selling on individual stocks.
- Another risk is that the broker may not have shares available for you to short the stock.
- Another situation that we have not yet considered: downward market momentum.

Currently the short-selling systems that we have presented are mean reversion systems. Mean reversion short systems require an overbought situation as the setup, in order to sell short (that is where we get the big edge).

What if that overbought situation does not happen?

What if the market sells off and it keeps going down? This can and did happen in the crashes of 1929 and 1987.

The market could literally keep falling and we would have no position in it—no ability to make a short-side profit to offset the losses were are experiencing on the long side. We'd be without any short position because there would be no setups—no overbought situation in the first place for our mean reversion systems to take advantage of.

The chance that this will happen is maybe not that high, but when it does happen you will regret not being prepared.

This brings us to the last leg of the suite:

Long-Term Trend Following Short

This system sells short when the market is in a downtrend and shows clear down momentum. We then jump on; as the market keeps selling off, we profit big-time with this system.

However, most people do not like a trend following short system because the results look terrible on a backtest (since we have a bullish sample size, and this profits in big downturns).

To appreciate the value of this system, change your mindset. Instead of expecting this system to make money regularly, think of it like health insurance: something that costs you a little money, and which you hope never to use. But if you need it, you're really glad you have it.

Remember that we backtest on results that favor long momentum systems, but the future can and will be different. We need a system that is our insurance policy. On the current backtest sample, a long-term trend following short system is a net loser, and most likely will be in live trading. But when a really catastrophic event happens you will be glad that you are in it.

We should not care about the single performance of this system because the objective of this particular system is not to be a net winner. **The objective is to make money in a specific market situation where the long systems will be guaranteed to be losers and the mean reversion short systems might not be in the market.**

See this small annual loss as a healthcare premium: you pay the price each year but know if something really bad happens you are covered.

System 7: The Catastrophe Hedge

- **Objective:** A system that sells short when the market shows down momentum that guarantees us being in a short position. It must be a very liquid instrument, and preferably that instrument is replicated by a derivative in case it is not shortable. The key objective for this system is to make money when the market goes down in full momentum.
- **Beliefs:** There will be times when the markets sell off with such momentum that we need a system to protect us in this downward move. During our lifetime we will see some catastrophic events in the stock market, and we need to be prepared for those. We need insurance for our long exposure. This system does not work in most market types, only in

the extreme down moves—so the individual performance of this system is irrelevant.

- **Trading Universe:** SPY (ETF of the S&P 500)
  - This is one of the most liquid instruments.
  - In case of a crazy moment that it is not shortable, we can use various derivatives like futures or options that would have an equal directional move.
- **Filter:** None
- **Setup:** The close of the SPY is the lowest close of the last fifty days
- **Ranking:** None
- **Entry:** Next day market on open
- **Stop-Loss:** three ATR of the last forty trading days
- **Profit Protection:** We stay in the short position until the SPY's close is the highest close of the last seventy days, then we exit next day market on open
- **Profit Taking:** None
- **Position Sizing:** For this example I have chosen a simple 100 percent of our total equity since it is only one symbol (we will not use 100 percent of our total equity in the combined suite).

As already mentioned, the results look terrible at first sight, but so does your spending on health insurance for the last twenty-four years!

Table 25: Results for The Catastrophe Hedge

January 2, 1995 – July 24, 2019	Trading System	SPY
CAGR%	-4.81%	8.02%
Maximum Drawdown	70.24%	56.47%
Annualized Volatility	11.97%	18.67%
Sharpe	-0.40	0.43
MAR	-0.07	0.14
Total Return	-70.17%	562.51%

Without understanding the conceptual thinking behind this system, you'd ask, "what good does a system like this do?" But let's take a look at the equity curve:

Chart 36: Equity Curve for The Catastrophe Hedge

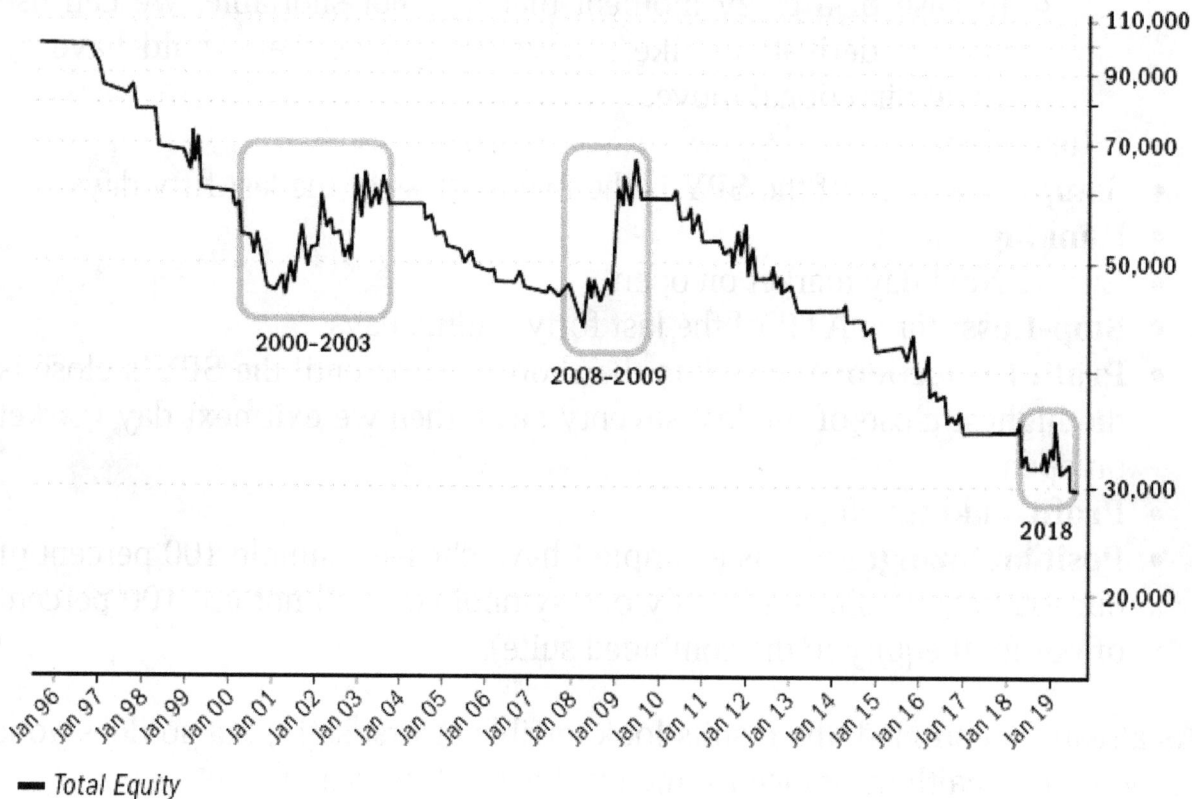

— Total Equity

In the rounded squares you see exactly when it makes money: In times of crisis.

Let's take this one step further and test this system a lot further back, all the way from 1927. We can't use SPY for that (the ETF didn't exist then), so we have used the S&P 500 index.

Chart 37: Equity Curve for The Catastrophe Hedge, 1927-2019

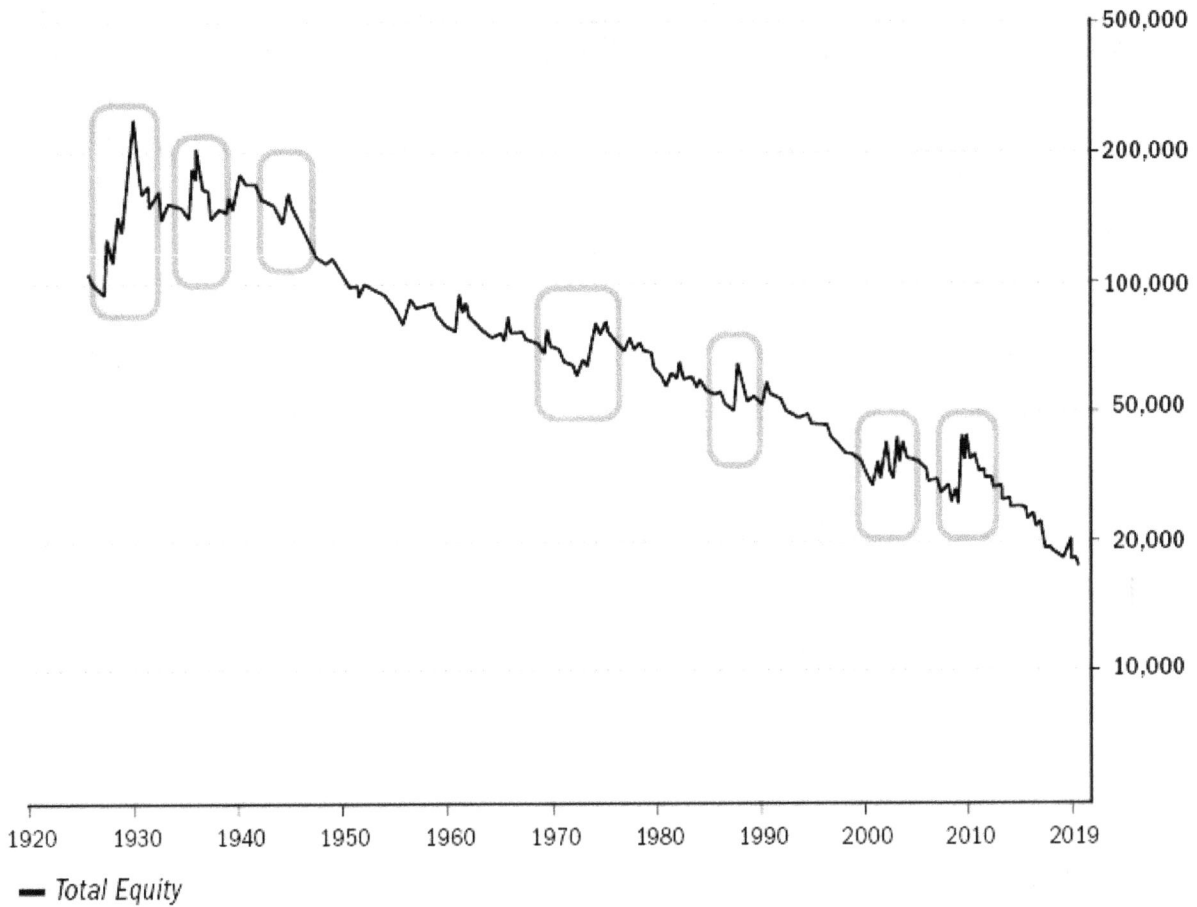

— Total Equity

Again, we see the same pattern: it loses money until it really needs to make money.

Let's look at some actual numbers. Best fifteen trades:

Table 26: Best 15 Trades, Catastrophe Hedge

Entry Date	Entry Fill	Exit Date	Exit Fill	Profit, %
1931.04.16	15.98	1932.03.07	8.82	44.2
2008.06.23	1,318.00	2009.05.04	907.24	30.4
1937.09.02	15.36	1938.06.23	11.03	27.7
1973.11.15	102.43	1975.01.28	76.03	25.8
1929.10.22	28.27	1930.02.05	23.31	17.9
2000.10.09	1,402.03	2001.12.06	1,167.10	16.5
1941.10.08	9.98	1942.06.05	8.37	16.0
1987.10.13	314.52	1988.02.22	265.64	15.7
1932.04.01	7.18	1932.08.01	6.11	14.6
1946.07.16	17.97	1946.12.20	15.50	13.7
1940.05.11	11.80	1940.08.12	10.38	12.0
1962.04.13	67.90	1962.11.15	59.97	11.7
1957.08.07	47.03	1958.01.30	41.68	11.4
1930.09.26	19.43	1931.02.11	17.28	10.9
2002.06.04	1,040.69	2003.05.05	926.55	10.6

Table 27: Most Profitable Years, Catastrophe Hedge

# Trades	Year	Gain, %
1	1931	36.40
1	2008	31.80
1	1974	27.00
3	1937	26.20
1	1929	19.10
3	1930	19.00
1	1987	18.00
2	1941	12.90
1	1957	12.00
1	2001	10.20
2	1962	9.30
3	1946	8.10
1	2018	7.00
2	1973	5.90

As you can see, this system can be incredibly useful when we most need it. But it has its price. There will be many losing years. In fact, on the backtest only 14 percent of the trades are winners. The rest are losers. Most of the years it will have a negative return.

Our strategy is to combine this with our existing suite of six systems. In this example I have chosen an allocation of 20 percent of our equity, reducing some allocation to the MR short systems and moving that money to the LTTF short Catastrophe Hedge system.

I'd be comfortable with a number like this because when the market falls with the kind of momentum we saw in 1929, 1987, or 2008, many but not all of our long positions will be closed out. We do not need to allocate too much to the Catastrophe Hedge because we are not fully exposed on the long side.

All Seven Systems Together

The charts below show the combined results of all seven systems, with the Catastrophe Hedge included. Here's how we allocated equity among the systems:

- Four long systems
  - Two trend-following
    - System 1: Long Trend High Momentum (25 percent of trading capital)
    - System 4: Long Trend Low Volatility (25 percent of trading capital)
  - Two mean reversion
    - System 3: Long Mean Reversion Selloff (25 percent of trading capital)
    - System 5: Long Mean Reversion ADX Reversal (25 percent of trading capital)
- Three short systems
  - Two mean reversion systems:
    - System 2: Short RSI Thrust (40 percent of trading capital)
    - System 6: Short Mean Reversion High Six-Day Surge (40 percent of trading capital)
  - One trend-following system
    - System 7: Catastrophe hedge (20 percent of trading capital)

Table 28: Results for Seven Systems Combined

January 2, 1995 – July 24, 2019	Trading System	SPY
CAGR%	30.44%	8.02%
Maximum Drawdown	11.83%	56.47%
Annualized Volatility	11.22%	18.67%
Sharpe	2.71	0.43
MAR	2.57	0.14
Total Return	68,115.39%	562.51%

Compared to the combined performance of six systems that I showed at the end of chapter 9, we see a hit in CAGR, although not much more drawdown because the mean reversion systems did so well in the bear markets.

If we ever end up in another catastrophe, or a time when stocks are not shortable, or pure down momentum scenarios like 1929–1932 or the 1987 crash, you'll be glad you included the Catastrophe Hedge in your combination of trading systems.

Conclusion

If you've read this far, you understand that the kind of investment performance I'm describing is not smoke and mirrors. It's achievable with self-knowledge, discipline, and the commitment to build systems you will trade consistently. The trading strategy of building combined, noncorrelated systems that I have described in this book reduces pain and anxiety, increasing your ability to stay in the market and achieve your financial goals, which should support your life goals.

Trading multiple noncorrelated systems in an automated way with end-of-day data has many, many benefits. In my experience, and that of my students, these are among the most important:

- You do not need to sit behind the screen the whole day. You enter orders each day before the market opens, which, depending on the number of multiple systems you trade, will take you anywhere from ten minutes to an hour a day.
- Once you have done the work of building your systems to suit your style, situation, and risk tolerance, you can let your computer do the work and simply execute the trades. The vast amount of your trading work becomes automated, freeing you to live your life.
- You do not need to watch the news or check newspapers.
- You do not need to be worried about the economic state of the country, because you make money when the economy is good or bad.
- You pay no attention to the fundamentals of the companies you trade in. In other words, all the daily noise about which stock has great prospects or is in trouble is irrelevant. Tune it out!
- You actually will have a life, because you are not glued behind screens, not worried about economics, Fed warnings, profit warnings, or anything else. You follow the trading system's computerized directions

before the market opens, and the rest of the day you do what you want.

- Because you have built systems you understand and believe in, you experience no anxiety around trading. You worry much, much less about what the market is doing—in fact, market behavior is almost irrelevant.
- You have the ability to make money in bull, bear, and sideways markets —again, leading to peace of mind and absence of anxiety.
- You can make consistently double-digit, yearly returns, with the scale of those returns correlated to your risk tolerance.
- Your drawdowns will be significantly lower than those of the markets (once more, reducing your anxiety). Remember, the S&P 500, Warren Buffett, and many others have all had drawdowns more than 50 percent. Depending on your risk level, you can attain big, market-beating returns without even beginning to come close to those large drawdowns. Your drawdowns could be easily three times lower, and you are still beat the market.

In the end, the approach I have described in this book simply delivers peace of mind. It's not easy at first. There is a lot of hard work. But the payoff is an enormous comfort with your trading and the freedom to live your life instead of worrying about your money.

You can't do this halfway. You have to stick with it, and you *will* have down periods. Most traders fail because they lose their nerve and get out when the pain is too great.

If you understand the concepts I have explained and are skilled with programming, I urge you to follow what I have described and build your systems yourself. You truly can succeed as a trader, as I have experienced and my students have, too.

However, for many people doing all this yourself can be complex and very time consuming. It could take years of trial and error. If you need help building your systems according to your beliefs, your risk tolerance and your goals, with the end result being a suite of trading systems that, once done take you only thirty minutes a day to execute (or even can be automated), I do mentor a select group of the people who I believe are the smartest traders.